Touch and Go

A comedy

Derek Benfield

Samuel French — London
New York - Toronto - Hollywood

ISBN 978-0-573-11301-7
www.samuelfrench-london.co.uk
www.samuelfrench.com

FOR AMATEUR PRODUCTION ENQUIRIES

UNITED KINGDOM AND WORLD EXCLUDING NORTH AMERICA

plays@SamuelFrench-London.co.uk

020 7255 4302/01

Each title is subject to availability from Samuel French,

depending upon country of performance.

TOUCH AND GO

First presented by Kimbrell Stepham Associates and Mark Furness at the Wyvern Theatre, Swindon, on 20th April, 1982, with the following cast:

Wendy	Suzi Jerome
Brian	Henry McGee
Hilary, Brian's wife	Jan Hunt
George	Trevor Bannister
Jessica, George's wife	Margaret Ashcroft

Directed by Charles Savage
Setting by Alan Miller-Bunford

The play takes place in two flats: one belonging to George and Jessica, and the other to Brian and Hilary. The flats are about two miles apart.

ACT I   A Wednesday evening in the Spring

ACT II   The following morning and the same evening

Time—the present

COPYRIGHT INFORMATION

(See also page ii)

Other plays by Derek Benfield published by Samuel
French Ltd:

Anyone for Breakfast?
Bedside Manners
Beyond a Joke
A Bird in the Hand
Caught on the Hop
Don't Lose the Place!
Fish Out of Water
A Fly in the Ointment
Flying Feathers
In for the Kill
Look Who's Talking!
Murder for the Asking
Off the Hook
Panic Stations
Post Horn Gallop
Running Riot
A Toe in the Water
Up and Running
Wild Goose Chase

ACT I

The living-rooms of two flats, one belonging to George and Jessica, the other to Brian and Hilary. The flats are about two miles apart. A Wednesday evening in Spring

The stage is in two halves: George and Jessica's flat is R and Brian and Hilary's flat is L. They are contrasting in design and furnishings: George and Jessica's being modern—white brick and stripped pine; while Brian and Hilary's is tasteful Victorian

The front doors of both flats are UC, and as you come into the modern half there are the first few steps of a staircase leading up and off to the R. An archway UR leads to the bathroom and a door further DR leads out to the kitchen. Below the kitchen door is a small built-in padded seat. There is a two-seater sofa RC with a low coffee table below it and a crescent table against the wall above the kitchen door. In the wall between the stairs and the archway are recessed shelves on which are various books, ornaments and a stereo music-centre. On one shelf are the drinks

In the other flat, a door in the corner UL leads to the bedroom and another door DL leads out to the kitchen. There is a cupboard against the wall between these doors on which, amongst other things, is a framed photograph of Brian. There is a small Victorian sofa LC with a low oval table in front of it, and an upright chair below the kitchen door. There is an antique chest against the wall UL with a window above it and a leopard skin hangs on the wall R of the window. There is an umbrella stand near the front door. (See groundplan on page 101)

There are two small telephone tables, one belonging to each flat, adjoining each other UC. Both flats are tastefully furnished with attractive ornaments and pictures, and each is carpeted in a different colour. Appropriate theme music is played before each act and at various times throughout the play

The Lights come up in George and Jessica's flat. The music continues until Brian's entrance

Wendy comes in from the bathroom. She is a very pretty girl and is carrying a perfume atomiser. She checks her appearance in the mirror on the wall, sprays her neck with the perfume and then, with a few sweeping balletic movements, sprays the air also. She smiles, happily, apparently satisfied with her preparations, looks at her wrist-watch, goes to put the front door on the catch and then disappears into the kitchen

A pause

Then the front door bursts open and Brian, in a bright red track suit, practically falls into the room

The music stops. He staggers to the sofa and collapses on to it, trying to regain his breath

Wendy returns with an ice-bucket. She sees Brian and smiles, delightedly

Wendy Hullo, Brian!

Without looking at her, Brian raises one hand and waves to her, breathing heavily. She grins, obviously quite used to him arriving in this state. She goes and mixes two gin-and-tonics, smiling to herself at the state he is in. Finally, she moves to him with the drinks. She holds one glass out to him and clinks the ice in it. Without looking up, Brian automatically holds one hand out towards her, a practised ritual. She puts the glass into it. He drinks deeply and without ceremony. She watches him patiently for a moment

Well? Aren't you going to take your clothes off?

Brian looks at her for the first time

Brian Give me a chance. I haven't got my breath back yet.
Wendy Well, if you don't get it back soon it'll be time for you to go home again before you've even had your drink, let alone anything else.
Brian Don't go mad. There's plenty of time.

Wendy Oh, good. Because, let's face it, you do *need* plenty of time. (*She sits down with her drink*)
Brian (*defensively*) Have I ever failed? Go on—tell me that! Have I ever failed?

She hesitates doubtfully

Wendy Well, it's been touch and go *some*times.

He glares at her in masculine outrage

Brian I beg your pardon?
Wendy It happens to everybody. (*She disappears into her gin*)
Brian Not to *me*! Never!
Wendy Twice.
Brian Twice?
Wendy To my certain knowledge.
Brian Ah! Wait a minute. You're not counting November, are you?
Wendy You said never. Never is not what it was.
Brian November was exceptional.
Wendy That's what I'm saying. It was touch and go. In November.

He gets up and goes grimly to refill his glass

Brian I remember the *two* occasions very well.
Wendy So do I! (*She giggles noisily into her glass*)
Brian (*infuriated*) It wasn't as bad as all that! (*He waits for her confirmation, but gets none*) The first time—if you remember—the central heating had failed. And the second time I'd lost my way in the park. Did you know that that night I'd run four miles by the time I got here?
Wendy (*giggling*) Yes. I could tell!

Brian hesitates, the gin bottle poised

Brian It was early days. I hadn't got used to the route, then. Is this our drink or George's?
Wendy It was over there.
Brian Then it's George's. (*So he helps himself more liberally*)

Wendy relaxes with her drink

Wendy I must say, it's very good of George to lend us his flat.
Brian (*logically*) Well, he's an old friend.
Wendy And that's what "old friends" are for?
Brian Certainly. Well, it's only once a week. And George plays darts on
a Wednesday evening, so he can spare us his pad for a couple of hours.
Wendy But what about his wife?
Brian Jessica?
Wendy *She* never seems to be here on a Wednesday, either.
Brian Ah—well, Jessica's a dress designer.
Wendy What's that got to do with it?
Brian She spends a lot of time abroad on business.
Wendy Lucky for us.
Brian Yes. Good old Jessica! (*He drinks*)
Wendy What about *your* wife?

Brian chokes on his drink

Brian (*nervously*) What?
Wendy *Your* wife.
Brian Hilary?
Wendy Is that her name?
Brian Yes.
Wendy Doesn't *she* suspect anything?
Brian Don't be silly. It was her idea.
Wendy (*surprised*) What?!
Brian "Too many business lunches", she said. "You'll have to do some
exercise." So I did.
Wendy I don't think she meant *this* sort of exercise!
Brian No, no—jogging! The jogging was her idea; this was my idea. (*He
chuckles*) I came home one night and there it was on the hall table.
Wendy (*puzzled*) Sorry?
Brian The track suit. This. She'd been out and bought it that morning. (*He
looks down at his track suit without enthusiasm*) H'm. Not quite my
colour but never mind. (*He sits on the sofa with his drink*)
Wendy And whenever you're here with me, your wife thinks you're
really jogging around the park?
Brian Why shouldn't she? I'm always exhausted when I get back! I say,
something smells good. Have you been cooking?

Wendy I *am* cooking. I thought it would be nice for us to have a meal
  together.
Brian (*glancing at his watch*) Do you think we've time for a meal?
Wendy (*disappointed*) I thought you'd be pleased.
Brian Well—yes—I am pleased, darling. Very pleased. It was a sweet
  thought. Very sweet. But we don't want to waste any time, do we?
Wendy I thought it would be romantic.

He looks at her blankly for a moment

Brian Romantic?
Wendy (*rather put out*) Don't you know the word?
Brian (*hastily*) Of course I know the word, darling. I'm as romantic as the
  next man, but——
Wendy But you'd sooner just get on with it! Is that it?
Brian Well ... well, I did think that was the idea, yes. You need to have
  time to be romantic. And we don't have a lot of that, do we?
Wendy Perhaps you ought to persuade George to play darts a bit longer,
  then! (*She moves away restlessly*)
Brian Yes. I'll have a word with him...
Wendy (*suddenly*) Coq au vin.
Brian I beg your pardon?
Wendy That's what we're having.
Brian Oh.
Wendy You don't like it.
Brian Yes, I do. I love it. Really. Love it.
Wendy But you don't want it?
Brian Well—you see—it isn't that I don't want it. It's just that—well, if
  I eat *now*...
Wendy Ah! I suppose your wife's keeping something for you! Is that it?
Brian Well...
Wendy Yes!
Brian Yes...
Wendy (*grimly*) I see.
Brian It would be surprising if she didn't. After all, as far as Hilary's
  concerned, I've been jogging around the park, haven't I?

She faces him, defiantly

Wendy There's no need for you to hang around here, then! You may as
  well go.

Brian (*plaintively*) But I haven't taken my clothes off yet...
Wendy You needn't bother. If you won't have my *coq au vin*, you're not
having me! (*She turns away from him*)

Brian gets up and moves towards the kitchen, irritated

Brian All right! All right! I'll have the *coq au vin*. Come on! We'll both
have the *coq au vin*. Let's go into the kitchen and have the *coq au vin*.
Wendy It's not ready yet.
Brian Good. Then there's time for another drink.

He stomps away to the drinks and refills his glass

(*Brusquely*) You want some more of George's gin?
Wendy (*icily*) If you can spare it.

*She holds her glass out to him, abruptly. He brings the gin and a bottle of
tonic water and refills her glass. They watch each other warily across the
glass as he does so. Then they begin to laugh. He leans forward and kisses
her. He surfaces after a moment. They have both enjoyed the kissing*

Brian (*enthusiastically*) H'mmmmm...

He struts back to get his own drink. She sits on the sofa

Wendy Do you sleep with her?

He stops and turns

Brian I beg your pardon?
Wendy Your wife. Do you sleep with her?
Brian We sleep in the same room, yes. We've been married for fifteen
years. It's not easy to break a habit like that.
Wendy I suppose it's not easy to break *other* habits, either.
Brian Don't be silly, now.
Wendy Well...
Brian You don't think I run two miles here, spend two hours with you,
run two miles back and then go for double top, do you?

They both laugh. He comes and sits beside her and speaks gently

I love you, stupid. Don't you know that?
Wendy (*sulking a little*) Once a week.
Brian I *see* you once a week. I don't stop loving you the minute I get back into my track suit.
Wendy (*cheering up*) Good...

She smiles. He leans towards her, ready to kiss. She grabs him and pulls him enthusiastically to her and they kiss. After a moment they emerge, looking at each other

Brian You go and turn off the *coq au vin*...
Wendy And you go and take off your track suit!

The theme music fades up as they race out of their appropriate doors: she to the kitchen, he to the bathroom; both giggling with anticipation

Black-out

The Lights come up in the other flat. The music continues until George appears

Hilary comes in from the bedroom. She is wearing a delightful and revealing dress and is carrying a perfume atomiser. She repeats, identically, the business that Wendy did, checking her appearance in the mirror, spraying herself with the atomiser and then spraying the room. She smiles, happily, apparently satisfied with her preparations, looks at her wrist-watch, goes to put the catch on the front door and then goes out to the kitchen

The front door opens slowly and George's head appears. He is out of breath. George is a pleasant, amiable man. He sees that all is clear and comes into the room, closing the door behind him. He is wearing a suit and a cap, yellow safety harness and yellow bicycle clips. He carries a bottle of red wine wrapped in paper and a bicycle pump, which he puts down in the umbrella stand. He moves carefully down into the room, breathing heavily. He puts the wine down, takes off his cap and harness, folds them up carefully and puts them into his pocket. He sits down on the sofa, gratefully

Hilary returns, stirring cocktails briskly in a glass jug. She sees him and smiles, delightedly

Hilary Hullo, George!

Without looking at her, George raises one hand and waves to her, still trying to regain his breath. He picks up the bottle of wine and holds it out to her. She takes it and puts it down next to Brian's photograph. She pours two martinis and returns to him. She looks at him for a moment, the drinks poised

Well? Aren't you going to take your bicycle clips off?

George laughs and takes off his bicycle clips. He puts them down on the table and accepts his cocktail. Hilary sits beside him and they look at each other, contentedly

Well—cheers!
George Yes, rather!

They drink. Then they put down their glasses. She grabs him, abruptly, and kisses him enthusiastically. After a moment, he surfaces breathlessly

Steady now. Don't go mad. There's plenty of time.
Hilary Are you sure?
George Of course I'm sure. Brian always jogs for two hours, doesn't he?
Hilary Yes. Usually. But two hours on the trot seems such a long time. Suppose he got tired and came back early?
George He won't. He's far too busy.
Hilary (*puzzled*) What?
George Jogging! You know—one, two; one, two; one, two!
Hilary (*playfully*) What would you do if he *did* come back early?
George He never has before. I know Brian. He always concentrates one hundred per cent whenever he's doing it.
Hilary H'm?
George Jogging! You know—one, two; one, two; one, two!
Hilary But suppose he did? What would you *do*?
George (*reassuringly*) Hilary, will you stop worrying? He won't come back.
Hilary Well, it looks like rain.
George He likes the rain.
Hilary I know my husband. If it rains he'll break off in the middle and come home.

George Oh, no, he won't! (*He chuckles*)
Hilary You can't be sure.
George Oh, yes, I can!
Hilary How?
George Never you mind. I just know. Trust me. I promise you. Brian
won't be back for at least two hours.
Hilary (*relieved*) Oh, good! Cheers!
George Cheers!

*They drink and snuggle down together, cosily, his arm around her. They
sigh happily*

Hilary It was certainly a great day.
George Today?
Hilary The day I bought Brian that track suit.
George Ah. Yes.
Hilary Bright red.
George Is it? Good Lord. Well, you could hardly miss that. (*He chuckles*)
Hilary I was walking past the shop and there it was.
Hilary ⎫
               ⎬ (*together*) Bright red!
George ⎭
Hilary So I went straight in and bought it. Mind you, red isn't really
Brian's colour.
George I don't suppose you notice. Not once you're on the trot. It was
lucky you knew his size.
Hilary Well, we have been married a few years now.
George Yes. I know. I was there.
Hilary Where?
George At the wedding.

She looks at him blankly

Hilary *Were* you?
George (*impatiently*) I was the best man!
Hilary Oh. Well, you've been promoted, haven't you?

They laugh

I'll get you another martini.
George What a good idea.

Hilary takes their glasses and goes to get fresh drinks

Hilary The moment I saw that track suit I thought, "Just the thing for Brian". I mean, he does need the exercise.
George Well, he's getting that all right!
Hilary What?
George Jogging! You know—one, two; one, two; one, two!

Hilary arrives with fresh martinis

Hilary Mind you, I hadn't thought of *this* when I thought of *that*!
George Hadn't you really? Good Lord. Not even after those evenings in my car with the windows steaming up? This is *much* more comfortable.
Hilary (*giggling*) Not so adventurous, though. (*She sits beside him*)

George drinks his martini quickly, then gets up and takes off his jacket

What are you doing?
George I'm taking my clothes off.
Hilary You said there was no hurry.
George Well, you *have* got a bit of a start on me. (*He glances at her* décolletage)

He folds his jacket up rather precisely and places it carefully on the sofa. Hilary watches him in amusement, and giggles

What are you laughing at?
Hilary You. You're so romantic.
George What?
Hilary Romantic! Don't you know the word?
George Oh. Yes. Rather. (*He reacts*) Me?
Hilary Folding your clothes up like that.
George Yes. (*Surveying his jacket*) Yes. It *is* rather sexy, isn't it? (*He takes off his tie*)
Hilary *Now* what are you doing?
George I'm taking my tie off.
Hilary You never took your tie off when we were in your car! (*She laughs*)

He gives her a look and puts his tie over the back of the sofa. Then he takes off his shoes and puts them down, ignoring her elaborately

What about Jessica?

George turns to look at her, nervously

George Who?
Hilary Your wife.
George Look—do we have to talk about her?
Hilary Why not? I like her.
George So do I. But I don't want to talk about her when I'm taking my clothes off.
Hilary When are you expecting her back from America?
George Not till tomorrow.
Hilary Oh, good! (*She sips her drink, contentedly*)

George starts to unzip his fly

Do you make love to Jessica in your car?

George hastily zips his fly up again, rather put out

George Of course I don't make love to Jessica in my car! She's my *wife*, isn't she? You don't make love to your own wife in your own car.
Hilary Somebody *else's* car?
George Not in a car at all!
Hilary Oh. Poor Jessica... (*She sips her drink*)

George has noticed the framed photograph of Brian

George And while we're on the subject——
Hilary What?
George Look at this! (*He picks up the photograph*)
Hilary What about it?
George Well, look at it!

She looks at it

Hilary It's Brian.
George I know it's Brian. That's the point. (*He replaces the photograph*) Couldn't you have removed it?
Hilary Why should I? He's my husband.

George (*patiently*) Yes. Yes, I know Brian's your husband. The point is, does *this* have to be *here*?

Hilary Where would you prefer it to be?

George I don't want it to be *any*where.

Hilary (*disappointed*) Oh... But this is where Brian lives.

George Hilary... Hilary, I—I know this is where Brian lives. I know that. But wouldn't it have been ... well—more tactful—to remove it?

Hilary (*astounded*) Remove my own husband's photograph?

George For the time being.

Hilary Why?

George What?

Hilary *Why?*

George Well ... (*he moves away from the photograph a little*) well, he's—he's looking at me.

Hilary He was looking at the camera so he's bound to be looking at you.

George He's looking at me ... disapprovingly.

Hilary How do you expect him to look at you when you're taking your trousers off? Oh, go on. Don't be silly. Get on with it.

George gives Brian's photograph a wary look, turns his back on it and starts to unzip his fly slowly. He sees Hilary watching him, so he tries to turn away from her as well. The task is hopeless. He zips his fly back up again

George It's no good! I can't get into the swing of it.

Hilary laughs and gets up

Hilary All right—I'll go and see to the dinner.

George Dinner? What dinner?

Hilary disappears, giggling, into the kitchen

George starts to follow her, then notices "Brian" still staring at him. He goes and picks up the photograph and speaks to it

Sorry, Brian. No hard feelings.

He puts the photograph face down and hastens towards the kitchen

Hilary!

George goes into the kitchen, anxiously

Black-out. The theme music fades up and continues until Wendy appears

The Lights come up in George and Jessica's flat

> *The front door opens and Jessica comes in. She is carrying a small suitcase, a handbag and a plastic bag from the duty-free shop. She closes the door and puts her luggage down, gratefully. She notices some letters, picks them up and looks at them*

> *Wendy comes in from the kitchen. She is now wearing an apron (belonging to Jessica). She stops in mid-stride when she sees Jessica. She does not know who she is*

Wendy Oh!

Jessica sees Wendy. She does not look at all surprised, and smiles cordially

Jessica Ah. Hullo.
Wendy Who the hell are *you*?

Jessica is a little taken aback by Wendy's direct approach

Jessica I beg your pardon?
Wendy What are *you* doing here?
Jessica I've just arrived.
Wendy How did you get in?
Jessica There's a door. Over there. It wasn't very difficult.
Wendy Oh, dear. He must have left it open.
Jessica No, no. I have my own key.
Wendy You do?
Jessica Well, I am over twenty-one. Don't look so worried. It's all my fault. I got back a bit sooner than you expected, didn't I?
Wendy You certainly did! (*She reacts*) Back from where?
Jessica From America, of course.

Wendy realizes who Jessica is

Wendy Oh, my God, it's *you*! (*She glances anxiously towards the bathroom*)

Jessica If I hadn't caught an earlier plane, I expect you'd have finished and gone home before I arrived.

Wendy Yes—that was the idea!

Jessica Have you got much more to do?

Wendy Quite a lot, yes...

Jessica glances around the room

Jessica I'd never have guessed. It all looks neat and tidy. Nothing lying about.

Wendy What *are* you talking about?

Jessica Well, he told me he'd get somebody in for a few hours occasionally while I was away.

Wendy looks astonished

Wendy He told you about *me*?

Jessica Well, he didn't say you specifically. I don't suppose he knew at the time who it would be. It would naturally depend on who was available.

Wendy Available?!

Jessica By the way, he's very forgetful sometimes. I do hope he remembered to pay you.

Wendy (*aghast*) He doesn't pay me!

Jessica He doesn't?

Wendy What do you think I am? I wouldn't take money from him.

Jessica Oh, I see. You're a friend and you do it for nothing? Well, it's very kind of you, but I shall insist that he pays you. How often have you been?

Wendy Er ... once a week.

Jessica How long for?

Wendy Oh ... a couple of hours. Except when he gets lost in the park, then we have to rush it a bit.

Jessica (*puzzled*) I beg your pardon?

Wendy 'Course, if the central heating fails we can't rush it at all! (*She giggles self-consciously*)

Jessica looks rather bewildered

Jessica I think I need a drink.

She goes and pours herself a gin-and-tonic

I say, there's a lovely smell of cooking. You don't prepare food for him as well, do you?
Wendy This is the first time. We were going to eat together afterwards.
Jessica (*coming down with her drink*) Oh, how nice! What did you say your name was?
Wendy Wendy.
Jessica Hullo, Wendy. (*She shakes the astonished Wendy by the hand*) What time are you expecting him back, then?
Wendy I'm not expecting him. He's already here.
Jessica Here? Really? Oh, good! I hadn't phoned him about my early plane, so I thought he'd probably be out. (*She sits on the sofa*) Where is he, then?
Wendy In the bathroom.
Jessica What's he doing in the bathroom?
Wendy Taking his clothes off, of course.

Jessica naturally looks a little surprised

Jessica It's not like him to take his clothes off when the cleaning lady's still here...

Wendy stares at her in amazement

Wendy Cleaning lady?!
Jessica Isn't that what you're here for? To clean the flat?
Wendy Er—no. Not exactly.
Jessica Then what the hell are you doing in here, dressed like that, when my husband's out there taking his clothes off?
Wendy Your *husband*?
Jessica Yes! George!

Whereupon Brian comes in from the bathroom. He has now removed his track suit and is wearing a splendid dressing gown and red socks. He does not see Jessica

Brian Well, here I am! (*He pirouettes to show himself off to Wendy*) What do you think of that?
Jessica Oh, very sexy indeed.

Brian now sees Jessica. He freezes, staring at her, unable to think what to say. Jessica looks back at him with a smile that could slice bacon

Hullo, Brian. What a *lovely* surprise...!
Brian Jessica!
Jessica Right first time.

Brian gives a nervous laugh

Brian I... I expect you're wondering what I'm doing here.
Jessica Well ... yes. It had crossed my mind.

Brian glances at Wendy

Brian I take it you two have met?
Jessica Oh, yes. We've met all right! We've been having a very interesting conversation.
Wendy (*to Jessica*) You must be very surprised to see *him* here.
Jessica Yes—I am!
Wendy I expect *you* thought he'd be running around the park.

Jessica looks blank. Then she looks at Brian

Jessica Not dressed like that, surely?
Brian (*weakly*) My track suit's in the bathroom.
Jessica Why on earth did you take it off?
Brian Ah—yes—well, there was a very good reason.
Jessica (*coldly*) Yes. I bet there was!

Brian turns to Wendy again, embarrassed

Brian Would you go and turn the *coq au vin* back on again?
Jessica *Coq au vin*? Is that what you're having?
Brian It was *her* idea.
Jessica That doesn't surprise me.

Wendy, highly embarrassed, turns to Brian

Wendy Look, I don't think——
Brian (*irritably*) Just turn the gas back on!

*He pushes her out into the kitchen and returns reluctantly to Jessica.
Jessica looks at him severely. He cringes a little*

This ... er ... this isn't quite what it looks.
Jessica Oh, Brian, I'm so glad. Because, let's face it, it doesn't look good, does it?
Brian I mean, there really is a perfectly simple explanation.
Jessica Yes. I'm sure there is. (*Thinking hard*) Let's see now... You were running around the park in your blue track suit when——
Brian (*correcting her nervously*) Red.
Jessica What?
Brian Red. It's a red track suit.
Jessica (*looking at him thoughtfully*) I wouldn't have said that red was your colour, Brian.
Brian No, no, it isn't! You're right! It isn't!
Jessica I can just imagine you charging through the trees in red. You must look like a fire engine.
Brian Yes. I'd have preferred blue.
Jessica Then why didn't you *get* blue?
Brian It was Hilary. *She* bought the track suit.
Jessica (*considering deeply*) I wonder why she chose red... Ah! Perhaps she thought that if you ever got lost in the park it would be easier to find you if you were in red?
Brian (*weakly*) Do you suppose George would mind if I had another gin?
Jessica Help yourself.
Brian Thank you. (*He plods away to get a large gin*)
Jessica Well, Brian?
Brian H'm?
Jessica You said there was a perfectly simple explanation.
Brian Ah. Yes. That's right.
Jessica Well, what is it?
Brian What is it? Yes. (*He returns with his drink, thinking hard*) Er— well—you see, Hilary bought me the track suit because——
Jessica The red one?

Brian Yes. Because she thought it would be a good idea if I took up jogging. You know what jogging is?
Jessica Yes, Brian. I know what jogging is. It's just that I've never seen it done indoors before.
Brian Anyway—that's what I did. I took up jogging. And that's where I was tonight. Jogging around the park.

He takes a swig of gin-and-tonic, as if he had completed his explanation. Jessica waits patiently

Jessica Brian—that doesn't explain how you came to be here in my husband's dressing-gown in the company of a sexy young girl with a penchant for *coq au vin*.
Brian Ah. No. Well, I'm coming to that.
Jessica Good.
Brian Well, there I was—jogging. Quite quickly, actually. About five miles an hour, I should think. And I suddenly came round a corner beside a large tree. I think it was an oak tree. Yes, it was! Because it was wearing acorns. So that *would* be an oak tree. And that was where it all happened.
Jessica Where what all happened?
Brian That was where I fell.
Jessica Fell?
Brian Yes.
Jessica Fell over the oak tree?
Brian Not *over* the oak tree. I fell *under* the oak tree. I must have tripped.
Jessica Over the acorns.
Brian Possibly, yes. Anyway, I fell face down in the water.

Jessica looks puzzled

Jessica You never mentioned water.
Brian Didn't I?
Jessica No.
Brian Ah—well—yes, there was water.
Jessica What sort of water?
Brian Wet water.
Jessica (*patiently*) Yes, but was it moving, or still?
Brian Oh—still. Until I fell in it, then it was moving.
Jessica Oh, I see! A pond?

Brian Exactly! And that's where I fell—into the pond. I was quite badly
  bruised. I was black and blue.
Jessica Black and red.
Brian What?
Jessica Well, the track suit was red.
Brian Not any more. It was covered in mud. I was in a terrible state.
Jessica I'm sure you were. And what happened then?
Brian Well, the most extraordinary thing. I was lying there, soaking wet,
  when all of a sudden—and you're going to find this very difficult to
  believe—all of a sudden ... along came Wendy.
Jessica Wendy?
Brian Yes.
Jessica *This* Wendy?
Brian Yes.
Jessica How on earth did she find you? Had you tied a yellow ribbon
  round the old oak tree?
Brian She was just walking through the park.
Jessica What a bit of luck!
Brian Yes, that's what *I* thought. Fancy tripping over a tree in the park
  and the next minute along comes the Red Cross.

Jessica considers this for a moment

Jessica The Red Cross?
Brian Yes. Wendy. She's a nurse with the Red Cross.
Jessica Of course. How silly of me! I should have known. She's wearing
  the new uniform.
Brian So that was that.
Jessica What was what?
Brian Help was on hand. Fortunately. So the first thing to do was to get
  that track suit off as quickly as possible.
Jessica Under the oak tree.
Brian No, no, no! I couldn't take it off in the middle of the park, could
  I? And then—suddenly I remembered that you and George lived *here*!
  Quite close to the pond.
Jessica How very fortunate. So Florence Nightingale brought you back
  here?
Brian Well, I thought it was the best thing to do. Under the circumstances.
Jessica I'm sure you did. It was such a pity that George wasn't in.
Brian Ah—well, it was his darts night, wasn't it?

Jessica I didn't know George played darts.

Brian looks at her in mock disbelief

Brian You *didn't?* George is in the first team at the *Coach and Horses!*
Jessica So how did you get in?
Brian (*blankly*) What?
Jessica Into the flat. When you found George wasn't here.
Brian With the key, of course.
Jessica What key?
Brian The one outside. George always puts a spare key under the geraniums by the front door. In case of emergency.
Jessica And this was certainly one of those!
Brian You mean you didn't know about the spare key?
Jessica No. Still, *you* knew. And that was the main thing. So you let yourselves in and took off your wet clothes?
Brian Yes.
Jessica And how did the *coq au vin* get here? Meals on wheels?

Wendy returns from the kitchen

Wendy Well, I'm all ready! Brian, are you going to serve?

Jessica laughs. Brian gives her a wary look

(*To Jessica*) And you don't have to worry. There's plenty for you as well.

Jessica gets up and collects her handbag

Jessica No, no. I really mustn't interrupt you both any longer.
Brian You're not going, are you?
Jessica (*a little frosty*) Oh, yes, Brian. I think so.
Brian But you live here! You've just arrived!
Jessica Well, *I'm* not in the mood for *coq au vin*. I think I'll go and find George. Nice to have met you, Wendy. I don't expect you'll be here when I get back. I know how busy you nurses are.
Wendy (*puzzled*) What?
Jessica (*to Brian*) The *Coach and Horses*, did you say?
Brian What?

Jessica The darts match.
Brian Ah—yes.
Jessica I think I'll pop in and give George a surprise.
Brian Mind you don't put him off his treble! (*He chuckles*)
Jessica (*heading for the front door*) You'll put the key back where you found it, won't you?
Brian Yes—rather!
Jessica I do hope your track suit dries out all right.

Wendy looks at Brian. He avoids her questioning eyes

And as for your bruises—I'm sure I can safely leave you in the hands of the Red Cross.

Jessica smiles, sweetly, at Wendy and goes out, closing the door behind her

Wendy What's she talking about?
Brian Never mind. It's a long story. (*He starts for the kitchen*)
Wendy Where are you going? The bedroom's up there.
Brian Yes, but the *coq au vin*'s down here. You said it was ready.
Wendy It can wait. It's only on a low gas. (*She smiles, sexily*) Let's work up an appetite first...
Brian (*retreating*) No! No! (*Unhappily*) I don't think I could. Not now...

Brian disappears into the kitchen

Wendy (*following him, forlornly*) Don't tell me your central heating's failed again?

Black-out

The Lights fade up in the other flat

George is pulling Hilary in from the kitchen

George Come on! Don't let's waste any more time!
Hilary What?
George Well, I was a bit later than usual getting here tonight.

Hilary Yes, you were! Why was that?

George I had a puncture.

Hilary I can't think why you have to come here on a bicycle, anyway.

George I could hardly leave my car parked outside, could I? Somebody might see it.

Hilary And what if they see a bicycle?

George They'll think you're having it away with the window-cleaner.

They laugh

Hilary All right, then. We'd better have it now.

George (*enthusiastically*) That's what *I* thought!

She prepares to go. He starts to unzip his fly again. She stops and looks at him with a smile

Hilary George!

George What?

Hilary Food.

George Food?

Hilary Food first.

George We don't usually have food.

Hilary This is a special occasion.

George Is it? I didn't know that. What special occasion?

Hilary We've been doing this every Wednesday for three months.

George (*impressed*) Have we really? Good Lord. We must be getting the hang of it by now.

Hilary So I cooked you a meal.

George What a sweet thought.

Hilary *Coq au vin.*

George Sorry?

Hilary That's what we're having.

George *Coq au vin?*

Hilary You don't like it.

George Yes, I do. I love it. Really. Love it.

Hilary Good.

George But are you ... are you sure we've got time for all that?

Hilary All what?

George Well ... food—and afters.

Hilary Oh, yes! I'll keep an eye on the clock.
George Will you? Oh...
Hilary (*grinning*) Not *all* the time, silly!
George Oh, good.
Hilary I've cooked quite a lot.
George (*fearfully*) Have you? Oh, dear. I'm not really very hungry.
Hilary That's all right. I want to leave some for Brian.
George Do you?
Hilary Well, yes, of course. He's bound to be hungry after all that jogging.
George (*considering*) Yes. Yes, I suppose he will...
Hilary I'll go and serve up. We don't want to waste any *more* time, do we?
  You get ready.
George Right.

She kisses him lightly and fondly, and goes out to the kitchen

George finishes his drink quickly and unzips his fly again. He looks to make sure "Brian" is not watching, turns his back towards the face-down photograph to make sure, and takes off his trousers. He folds them neatly and puts them on top of his jacket

The doorbell rings

George freezes in horror

The doorbell rings again

  Hilary comes in from the kitchen

George clings on to her, alarmed

  The front door! There's somebody at the front door!
Hilary Oh, no!
George Oh, yes! He's back!
Hilary Who's back?
George Brian, of course! Your husband!
Hilary Don't be silly. It can't be Brian. He'd have a key.

The doorbell again

George Well, whoever it is, get rid of them! (*Glancing at his state of undress*) They can't see me like this!
Hilary Well, go and hide in the bedroom!
George Oh, my God...!

George is pushed out into the bedroom

Hilary dithers uncertainly for a moment and then goes and opens the front door

Jessica is standing there

Hilary Jessica!
Jessica (*smiling broadly*) Right first time.

A loud crash from inside the bedroom as George reacts nervously to hearing that it is Jessica. Jessica comes in, looking towards the bedroom

What on earth was that?
Hilary What on earth was what?
Jessica I heard something in the bedroom.

Hilary closes the front door and moves quickly to Jessica, her mind racing

Hilary Ah—yes. It's next door. The people next door.
Jessica What?
Hilary They're—they're practising.
Jessica (*puzzled*) Practising?
Hilary Yes. They're doing it in the square on Saturday!

Jessica looks blank

Morris dancing! Have you ever seen Morris dancing, Jessica? It's wonderful. You should try it sometime.

Without realizing, Hilary picks up George's tie from the back of the sofa and waves it about as she essays a modest Morris dance. Jessica watches in astonishment. Hilary suddenly realizes that she has George's tie in her

*hand and, as her dancing loses fire and slows down, and unseen by
Jessica, she rolls the tie up and pops it down her cleavage*

Jessica I hope you didn't mind my popping in like this.
Hilary Oh, no. Of course not. (*She glances, nervously, towards the
bedroom*)
Jessica You weren't in the middle of anything, were you?
Hilary No! It was just a bit of a surprise. I thought you were in America.
Jessica Yes, I was. I was coming back tomorrow.
Hilary That's what I thought!
Jessica But I came back today instead.
Hilary So I see. (*Wandering, with overdone casualness, towards the
bedroom*) What an exciting life you lead, Jessica! (*She stresses the name
each time for George's benefit*) It must be wonderful to be a fashion
designer, *Jessica*. Shooting about from place to place ... *Jessica*! (*She
returns a little*) Did George know you were coming back today?
Jessica No. It'll be quite a surprise for him.
Hilary It certainly will...!
Jessica What?
Hilary Would you like a dry martini?

Hilary goes out to the kitchen

Jessica Good heavens. How posh.

Hilary returns with a glass

Please don't bother. Anything will do.
Hilary I've got some mixed.
Jessica (*surprised*) Some martini?
Hilary Yes. Look!

*She picks up the jug, then notices Brian's photograph face-down, hastily
puts it upright and stirs the martini, noisily. Jessica is a little surprised by
Hilary's behaviour*

Jessica How very smart. *We* only have dry martinis on special occasions.
Hilary This *is* a special occasion.
Jessica Oh? Are you celebrating something?

A crash from the bedroom as George knocks something over, nervously. Hilary covers up quickly

Hilary Ah! There they go again! They're going to be in splendid form by Saturday.
Jessica H'm?
Hilary The Morris dancers. (*She does a brief dance*)
Jessica Oh. Yes. Of course.

Jessica is bewildered by Hilary's uncharacteristic behaviour. Hilary pours a martini and brings it to Jessica

Thank you. You never told me *what* you were celebrating.
Hilary Ah. No, I didn't, did I? Well—your homecoming, of course!

Jessica smiles, still a little puzzled

Jessica You mean you mixed martinis today ready for tomorrow?
Hilary I-er-I thought I'd better practise a bit tonight.
Jessica *Practise?*
Hilary Ready for tomorrow! I mean, after all, you've been to America. (*With an American accent*) And they sure know how to make martinis there, don't they, pardner?

Jessica looks at her, astonished. Then she raises her glass

Jessica Cheers!
Hilary Cheers!

Hilary raises her hand to drink, realizes that she has no glass and squeals, nervously

Aah! Now where did I put *my* glass?
Jessica Well, there are *two* over there.
Hilary (*alarmed*) What?! (*She goes and picks up the glasses that she and George had been using*)
Jessica (*watching her*) Have you been entertaining already?
Hilary Ah—yes—of course! I forgot. They—they popped in for a drink.
Jessica Who did?
Hilary The neighbours. Next door.

Jessica looks at her martini, having taken a sip

Jessica H'm. Delicious. Very strong.
Hilary Good. I'm glad you approve.
Jessica No wonder your neighbours started Morris dancing in the sitting-
room.

*They laugh. Hilary goes quickly with the two glasses, refills one for herself
and, unseen by Jessica, downs it in one and pours another. Jessica puts
down her drink and is about to sit on the sofa, but George's suit is there.
She picks it up, without recognizing it*

Shall I put this out of the way?

*Hilary turns and sees Jessica with George's clothes. She puts down her
glass, races to Jessica, takes the suit from her and hastily bundles it into
the chest*

Hilary Brian is *so* forgetful! He said he was taking that suit to the cleaners
this morning. Fancy leaving it lying about the place like that. So untidy.
What can the neighbours have thought? He really is dreadful.
Jessica (*sitting on the sofa*) Brian is obviously just like George.
Hilary Is he?
Jessica Oh, yes. George always folds up his clothes very neatly, too—just
like that. The minute he takes them off. (*She notices George's shoes on
the floor, and peers at them*)
Hilary Does he really? Good Lord...

Jessica picks up the shoes

Jessica Were the shoes supposed to go to the cleaners, too?
Hilary (*vaguely*) Shoes? (*She sees the shoes*) Shoes! (*She races across
to Jessica*) That was my fault! I promised to take them to be mended.

*She takes the shoes from Jessica, hides them awkwardly behind her, moves
backwards towards the chest, opens it without looking and drops the shoes
inside. She closes the lid, relieved. Jessica watches all this in some
astonishment. Hilary returns, trying to appear casual*

You ... you didn't go straight home, then? From the airport.

Jessica Oh, yes.
Hilary (*alarmed*) What?
Jessica Yes.
Hilary You *did* go straight home?
Jessica Yes. But George wasn't there. (*Thoughtfully*) I spoke to a cleaning lady and a Red Cross nurse, but they couldn't help me...
Hilary (*bemused*) I beg your pardon?
Jessica Sorry. I think I'm a bit jet-lagged.
Hilary Would you like another martini—(*hopefully*) or do you have to go home?
Jessica I think I'd like another martini.
Hilary (*disappointed*) Oh. (*Then brightly*) Right! (*She goes to refill their glasses*)
Jessica So I went to find George at the *Coach and Horses*.
Hilary The *Coach and Horses*?
Jessica He plays darts there, apparently.
Hilary (*innocently*) And ... er ... wasn't he there?
Jessica No. So as I wasn't far from here I thought I'd pop in and borrow your phone to ring home and see if the coast is clear.
Hilary What?
Jessica (*correcting herself quickly*) To see if George is back yet!
Hilary Well, I should give it a bit longer, if I were you...! (*She glances apprehensively towards the hidden George*) Have you had anything to eat?
Jessica No. I haven't got around to that yet.
Hilary (*seeing a way out*) Then you must have something here!
Jessica Oh, no, I couldn't possibly——
Hilary I insist. You must be starving. So have something to eat here. (*Loudly, for George's benefit*) You can help me—in the *kitchen*! That'll give *George* time to get *home*!
Jessica (*puzzled by her manner*) What?
Hilary From wherever he is!
Jessica I don't want to put you to any bother...
Hilary No bother. It's already cooked. (*She smiles proudly*) We're having *coq au vin*.

Jessica looks at her

Jessica I beg your pardon?
Hilary That's what we're having.
Jessica *Coq au vin*?

Hilary You don't like it.
Jessica Yes, I do. I love it. Really. Love it. (*With a secret smile*) It's just
a bit of a coincidence, that's all.
Hilary What?
Jessica Nothing! Nothing! Martinis and *coq au vin*, eh? You do live well
around here.
Hilary Well, Brian's out jogging, you see. Round and round the park. You
know—one, two; one, two; one, two!
Jessica Yes. I know... And you're going to feed him when he gets back?
Hilary Yes, of course. He always works up *such* an appetite when he's
doing it.
Jessica Yes, I bet he does!
Hilary It's very energetic, jogging.
Jessica Yes. I know.
Hilary It takes a lot out of him.
Jessica Does Brian *know* you're having *coq au vin* tonight?
Hilary No. It'll be a lovely surprise for him. So you must have some as
well.
Jessica But you must leave plenty for Brian!
Hilary Oh, it's all right. I cooked enough for three.
Jessica Good heavens, you must have known you were going to have a
visitor.
Hilary (*quietly*) Yes, I did... Come along! You can help me in the kitchen.
Jessica All right. (*She gets up*) Then I really *must* ring George.

They start to go

Hilary Would you take the bottle of wine, please, Jessica.
Jessica Yes, of course. (*She collects the wine and heads for the kitchen,
looking at the bottle as she goes*) Oh, that delicious Mâcon! It's our
favourite.

Jessica goes into the kitchen

Hilary goes quickly to the bedroom door and opens it

*George comes out. He is now wearing Brian's dressing-gown, which
has a leopard skin pattern on it*

Hilary (*whispering, urgently*) It's Jessica!

George (*whispering also*) Yes—I know!
Hilary She's in the kitchen. You'll have to be quick.
George (*a little hurt*) Why are you giving her my share of the *coq au vin*?
Hilary Well, *you* can't have it now, can you?
George And that's not the only thing I can't have!
Hilary Go on—quickly! I can't keep her out of here for long.
George Right. (*He is about to go*)
Hilary George——
George Yes?

She kisses him quickly

Oh. Thanks.

Hilary smiles and goes into the kitchen

George goes to get his clothes from where he left them. He stops in his tracks when he finds they have gone. He looks behind, around and under the sofa, getting into more and more of a state, unable to locate them. He cannot understand what has happened to them

Jessica and Hilary's voices are heard from inside the kitchen

Jessica (*off*) I'll go and fetch the dirty glasses.
Hilary (*off*) No! It doesn't matter! There's no hurry!

George panics. He dithers uncertainly for a moment, then he notices the leopard skin hanging on the wall. He hastens to it and drapes himself against it in suitably feline posture, confident that the leopard skin pattern of Brian's dressing-gown now renders him totally invisible

Jessica comes in from the kitchen and goes to collect the used glasses, not noticing George against the leopard skin

Seeing that Jessica is facing the other way, George abandons his attempt at camouflage, tip-toes to the front door, collects his bicycle pump and leaves quickly, closing the door behind him

Jessica hears the door close, and turns. She smiles, suspiciously

Hilary comes in, urgently, from the kitchen. She is wearing oven gloves

Jessica! Come and get your *coq au vin*!

She is relieved to see that there is no sign of George

Jessica (*going to her*) It really is kind of you. Are you *sure* you don't
   mind?
Hilary Of course not. You're very welcome. Come along! (*She turns to go*)
Jessica Hilary...

Hilary hesitates

Hilary Yes?
Jessica Did you know you've got a man's tie down your cleavage?

*Hilary looks quickly down at her cleavage in horror, screams, clutches
her bosom and runs back into the kitchen. Jessica follows her in surprise
as the Lights fade*

The Lights come up in the other flat

   *Brian is being pulled firmly and resolutely out of the kitchen by Wendy.
   He is resisting, manfully*

Wendy Oh, come on, Brian!
Brian Where are we going now?
Wendy Well, you've had your *coq au vin*, so now we're going to have
   "afters".
Brian Oh, no, we're not!
Wendy Don't be such a spoilsport. That's what we came here for.
Brian I know! But there isn't time now. Jessica might come back!
Wendy Well, you can lock the door, can't you? Then she'll have to ring
   the bell.

Brian is appalled at such a suggestion

Brian I couldn't do that.
Wendy Why not?

Brian I couldn't concentrate.
Wendy Well, it's such a long time till next Wednesday.
Brian (*unhappily*) Yes. I know. Don't remind me.
Wendy Well, come on, then!
Brian No! It's too late now. I'm not in the mood.
Wendy All right, then—same time tomorrow!
Brian (*alarmed*) What?
Wendy You'll have to borrow the flat again tomorrow, that's all.
Brian I can't do that!
Wendy (*playfully*) Well, I'm going to turn up here tomorrow, so you'd better arrange it.
Brian I couldn't possibly! What would George say?
Wendy Tell him what's happened. He'd understand. Or doesn't George go in for this sort of thing?
Brian George? Good Lord, no! George is only interested in darts and football. Good God! Is that the time? I should be halfway home by now.
Wendy (*with a big smile*) All right, then. See you tomorrow...
Brian (*fearfully*) You wouldn't do that to me?
Wendy Yes, I would! (*She closes to him*) Oh, come on. Five minutes. Then you'll run home twice as quick.
Brian After five minutes I wouldn't be able to run home at all! It's no good. I've got to go. We've *both* got to go. You tidy up the kitchen while I get back into my track suit.

Wendy accepts the inevitable and smiles resignedly

Wendy Oh, all right.

She goes into the kitchen

Brian looks at his watch. It is later than he thought

Brian Oh, my God...!

He goes, quickly, into the bathroom

The front door opens and George comes in. He is still in his shirt and socks, and wearing Brian's dressing-gown. He leans against the door, grateful for the sanctuary of his own flat, and cools his face with the bicycle pump

Wendy comes out of the kitchen with a tray and sees a strange man in his socks and dressing-gown

Wendy Good Lord! There's not *another* booking, is there?
George What?
Wendy If you're here to meet a girl, I wouldn't bother. George's wife is back.
George Yes—I know! (*He puts down the bicycle pump*)
Wendy Then I shouldn't hang about if I were you. (*She collects up the used glasses*)
George (*irritably*) I thought you'd have gone by now!
Wendy I'm just going! And *you* ought to think twice about staying here. His wife'll be back any minute!
George I *live* here!
Wendy What?
George I'm George! I live here!
Wendy Oh, dear—I am sorry. It's just that we've never met before. I mean—you're never here when *I'm* here, are you?
George No. That's the idea!
Wendy Well, I shan't be long. I'm just tidying up. We'll be gone in a second.
George We? You mean *Brian's* still here, as well?
Wendy Yes. He's in the bathroom.

George looks down in horror at the dressing-gown he is wearing and hastily removes it

Wendy heads for the kitchen with the tray of glasses, but hesitates in the doorway

Here—do you *always* play darts in a dressing-gown?

She goes into the kitchen

George rolls the dressing-gown up into a ball and looks about, uncertain of where to hide it

Brian comes out of the bathroom in his track suit. George pushes the dressing-gown up under his shirt, which gives the impression that he has a large stomach

Brian sees George

Brian George!
George Ah!

They face each other for quite a time. George shifts uncomfortably. Brian is puzzled by George's mode of dress. Eventually...

Good Lord, that *is* red, isn't it?

Brian looks down at his track suit

Brian Ah. Yes. Not quite my colour, I'm afraid.
George No. (*Pause*) Blue would have been better.

Another pause. Brian is fascinated by George's appearance

Brian I... I hope I didn't keep you out of the bathroom.
George (*blankly*) What?
Brian Well... I mean... (*He indicates George's bare legs*)

George glances down at his bare legs

George Oh, no. No.
Brian I just thought you might have been ... in a bit of a hurry.
George Oh, no. I've... I've only just arrived, as a matter of fact.

Brian, naturally, looks a little surprised

Brian You didn't arrive like that?
George Yes.
Brian Oh...
George On my bike.
Brian Dressed like that on your bike?
George Yes.
Brian You rode through the streets dressed like that?
George Some of the way, yes.
Brian Didn't anybody ... say anything?
George A few people pointed at me. Laughed a bit.

Brian I'm not surprised. Wherever are your clothes? I thought you were playing darts, not strip poker.

Brian turns away from George for a moment. George takes the opportunity to remove the dressing-gown from under his shirt and to shove it under the sofa. Brian turns back to George

How did you come to lose your clothes?

George (*blankly*) What?

Brian Well, you must have set off with some clothes on! You surely didn't go *out* dressed like that?

George No, of course not! What do you take me for?

Brian Well, what happened to them?

George (*apprehensively*) You really want to know?

Brian Yes!

George Well, I... I fell off my bike.

Brian Fell off your bike and lost your trousers?

George Yes. You see ... the wheels wouldn't go round.

Brian I beg your pardon?

George On the bike. They wouldn't ... you know. (*He mimes a wheel going round*)

Brian They wouldn't...? (*He repeats the mime*)

George No.

Brian Why not?

George My trousers were caught in the chain.

Brian (*laughing*) Good Lord! What a dreadful thing to happen! Lucky you were able to stop. You might have been wound up like a hairspring. So you fell off?

George I had no choice.

Brian And then you took your trousers off?

George Of course I took my trousers off! I couldn't come in here with a bicycle fastened to me, could I?

Brian And what about your shoes? Did you have to take *them* off, as well?

George I had to take *them* off before I could get my trousers off!

Brian You didn't have to take your jacket off, though.

George Yes, I did! I was getting very hot out there!

Brian You'll be getting hotter still if Jessica sees you. (*He sits on the sofa and then remembers*) Oh, my God! You haven't heard!

George What?

Brian Your wife came back early.
George Yes, I know...!
Brian Ah! She found you, then?
George Nearly!
Brian What?
George No. I don't think so...
Brian Didn't she find you in the pub?
George Oh, no.
Brian Then how did you know she was back?
George (*dithering*) Er—I—I—(*he sees Jessica's suitcase and points to it, gratefully*) I saw her suitcase! Over there. (*He goes to Brian, anxiously*) She didn't catch you at it, did she?
Brian Well, not exactly "at it", George.
George But she saw you and—er—(*indicating the kitchen*)
Brian Wendy.
George Wendy.
Brian Yes.
George Oh, my God!
Brian Jessica didn't *know* about our Wednesday arrangement, did she?
George Of course she didn't know about it! You don't think I'd tell her, do you? You know what women are like. They can't keep a secret. They mean to. But they can't.
Brian (*fearfully*) Can't they?
George No.
Brian You mean she'll tell ... other people—about me and—er—(*indicating the kitchen*)
George Wendy.
Brian Wendy.
George Yes.
Brian Oh, my God! You don't think she'd tell ... *mine*, do you?
George You can never tell. She wouldn't mean to. I mean, she wouldn't want to upset Hilary, would she? She and Hilary are friends. (*He smiles, contentedly*) So that's good news, isn't it?
Brian Is it? Oh. That's all right, then. (*He cheers up*)

Quite a pause, then...

George Mind you—sometimes when they get together—and talk—well, it all comes out, doesn't it?
Brian Does it? All of it?
George Sometimes.

Brian Then we'll have to keep them apart.

George Good idea!

Brian I say—you don't suppose Jessica is round at my place now, do you? Talking?

George (*suddenly remembering*) Oh, my God! Jessica!

Brian (*surprised*) What?

George Jessica! I'd better get some clothes on.

Wendy comes out of the kitchen, ready to go home

Wendy (*to Brian*) I thought you were in a hurry to go home?

Brian I was talking to George!

Wendy turns to George

Wendy Oh, George—I hope your wife didn't go and spoil your little game.

George (*guiltily*) what little game?

Wendy Darts!

George Oh, darts. No—no, she couldn't find me.

Wendy I don't see how she could miss you dressed like that. What happened to your clothes?

Brian He fell off his bike.

Wendy What?

Brian Never mind. It's a long story.

The telephone rings. Brian and George freeze. The telephone goes on ringing. Wendy sees that they are not going to answer it and goes towards the telephone

Wendy All right—I'll answer it.

The Lights come up in the other flat

Hilary is coming in with a mobile telephone

George and Brian panic

George ⎫
            ⎬ (*together*) No!
Brian ⎭

They race after Wendy, but she reaches the telephone first. She lifts the receiver and hands it to George, with a big smile

Wendy There...!

George hands it to Brian, with a big smile

George There...!

Brian hands it back to George, with a big smile

Brian There...!

George holds the telephone, nervously, and assumes a croaky voice

George Hullo...?
Hilary Is that you, George?
George Yes...
Hilary Oh, good. You're back, then?
George Yes...
Hilary I just wanted to be sure.
George Yes...
Hilary Are you alone?

A pause

George Yes...
Hilary Is everything all right?
George Yes...
Hilary I kept Jessica here as long as I could. To give you a chance to get home.
George Yes...
Hilary She went about five minutes ago.
George (*alarmed*) What?!
Brian Who is it?
George (*to Brian*) Jessica!
Brian (*alarmed*) Jessica!
Hilary (*surprised*) What?
George (*into the phone*) Jessica! I didn't know you were back from America.

Hilary (*puzzled by this*) George...?
George Are you speaking from a call-box?
Hilary Of course I'm not speaking from a call-box. I'm at home.
George You'll be home *soon*?
Hilary No, George. I'm at home *now*.
George You'll be on your way *now*?
Hilary George, you didn't fall off your bicycle, did you?
George What a lovely surprise!
Hilary *What?*
George I didn't expect you here until tomorrow.
Hilary Tomorrow?
George (*wildly*) Yes! Tomorrow night! Had you forgotten? It was all arranged for tomorrow night!

Hilary is surprised and delighted

Hilary At *your* place? Will that be all right?
George (*alarmed*) What?
Hilary Are you *sure* you're alone?
George Yes, but there's someone at the door! I shall have to go.
Hilary All right, darling. See you tomorrow, then. Same time as usual.

She puts down the mobile phone, collects the martini jug and goes into the kitchen, smiling happily. The Lights in her flat fade to black

George What? (*He realizes that she has gone, and replaces the receiver*)
Wendy Who was that?
George
Brian } (*together*) Jessica!
George Speaking from a call-box!
Wendy She's on her way, then?
George Yes. She'll be here any minute!
Wendy Come on, then, Brian! Let's get out of here before she arrives.
Brian Good idea!

They start to go, quickly

Thanks for the use of the flat, George.
George It was my pleasure.

Wendy I'm glad it was *some*body's.
Brian (*to George*) Same time next week?
George You bet!

Brian and Wendy go quickly out of the front door, closing it behind them

George realizes that he must do something about his appearance before Jessica gets back, and races out to the bedroom. He returns with pyjama trousers and his dressing-gown (the one Brian had been wearing). He pulls on the pyjama trousers as quickly as he can and puts on the dressing-gown. He grabs an apple and a book, puts on his glasses, races to the sofa and settles down in a hastily assumed air of relaxation, eating the apple and reading the book

The front door opens and Jessica comes in. She sees him and smiles delightedly

Jessica George...!

George looks suitably surprised

George Hullo, darling! What a lovely surprise!

Jessica closes the door and comes down to him

Jessica I've been looking for you everywhere. But I couldn't find you.
George Oh, good.

She kisses him cosily

Jessica You weren't in the pub.
George Yes.
Jessica No.
George Yes. Only sooner.
Jessica Ah. Before I got there?
George Presumably.

She moves away, taking off her coat

Jessica I didn't know you were good at games.

George Neither did I...!
Jessica I expect you've been practising.
George (*modestly*) Just a little, yes.

Jessica puts down her coat. He keeps a wary eye on her

Jessica Then I popped in to see Hilary. She gave me two dry martinis and some *coq au vin.*
George (*ruefully*) Yes. I know...!
Jessica What?
George Nothing, darling.
Jessica It was delicious. A pity *you* weren't there.
George I very nearly was!
Jessica What?
George I—I nearly popped in. After my darts match.
Jessica Oh, then I'd have seen you.
George Yes. I nearly popped in. You know—to see old Brian!
Jessica Brian wasn't there.
George (*overdoing the surprise*) Wasn't he? Good Lord!
Jessica No. He was out jogging.
George Ah. Yes. Jogging. He does that occasionally.
Jessica (*coldly*) And that's not *all* he does occasionally!

George leaps up nervously, uncertain how much Jessica knows about Brian

George Can I get you a drink?
Jessica I think I've probably had enough already. We had some wine, as well.
George (*outraged*) Wine? You drank the wine?
Jessica Yes. It was that delicious Mâcon that we get from the shop on the corner here.
George (*grimly*) Yes. I know the one. (*Then quickly*) They sell it everywhere!
Jessica Still, perhaps a nightcap.
George Whisky?
Jessica Fine. (*She sits on the sofa*)

He plods away to get two whiskies

But I don't want to keep you up too long.
George What?

She smiles

Jessica Well—I can see you're very keen to get to bed.

He glances at his clothes

George Oh—these? Yes. I... I Just thought I'd change. You know. It is
pretty late. After all. And I'm... I'm quite tired.

*He arrives with two whiskies and gives one to her. She smiles at him and
holds on to his hand*

Jessica You don't have to be so sheepish. After all, you are a red-blooded
male and I have been away for two weeks.
George (*doubtfully*) Yes. Cheers...
Jessica Cheers!

They drink

*He starts to move away from her, but she has him by the hand and pulls
him back*

Where are you going?
George Oh, I—I just thought I'd—I'd have a little walk.
Jessica Come and sit down.
George Right.

*Rather reluctantly he sits down, but is careful to leave a gap between them.
She smiles and closes in. He looks apprehensive*

Jessica You are pleased to see me, aren't you?
George Yes, darling—of course I'm pleased to see you.
Jessica I came home a day early.
George Yes. I know. I saw your bags over there. I'll help you to unpack.

He tries to get up, but she restrains him again

Jessica There's no hurry. We can do that in the morning. After all—I don't need my clothes *tonight*, do I?

She looks at him with a sexy smile

George looks apprehensive

The Lights fade as—

The Lights come up in the other flat

> *The front door bursts open and Brian falls in, breathlessly. He staggers to the sofa and collapses on to it, trying to get his breath back*
>
> *Hilary comes in from the kitchen with a glass of wine. She sees the state he is in*

Hilary You know, darling—I think you're doing too much of it.

Brian looks at her, blankly

Brian I beg your pardon?
Hilary You always get back so exhausted. Are you sure all this exercise is good for you?
Brian Oh, yes. I always feel much better afterwards.
Hilary It would be dreadful if you reached the halfway mark and had a heart attack.

Brian considers this appalling prospect

Brian Yes, it would, wouldn't it!
Hilary (*sipping her wine*) If you'd been back a bit sooner you'd have seen Jessica.
Brian Jessica? *Here?*
Hilary Yes.
Brian (*anxiously*) *George*'s Jessica?
Hilary Yes.
Brian I thought she was in America.
Hilary They do let you out occasionally.

Brian I didn't think George expected her back until tomorrow.

Hilary No. He didn't.

Brian She should have let him know, then he could have been at home. I mean, Wednesday is George's darts night.

Hilary (*innocently*) Really? I didn't know George played darts.

Brian Oh, yes. He does it every Wednesday. He never *used* to play. But he's been practising hard these last few months. He must be quite good at it by now.

Hilary (*without thinking*) Yes, he is! (*She laughs*)

Brian What?

Hilary (*correcting herself quickly*) Yes, I'm *sure* he is.

Brian Anyway, I expect he'll be back home by now.

Hilary (*without thinking*) Yes, he is.

Brian What?

Hilary I expect he is! I mean, you can't go on playing darts all night, can you? I do hope he's got some food in...

Brian George?

Hilary Yes. You must get awfully hungry playing darts, and he hasn't had any dinner.

Brian How do *you* know? He might have done. He might have picked up a pie in the pub.

Hilary Yes. I suppose so. Still, you're *much* luckier.

Brian Am I?

Hilary Yes. (*With relish*) I've got some food waiting for *you*.

Brian (*warily*) Food? Have you?

Hilary Of course I have. I made it specially. You must be starving after running all that way.

Brian's stomach churns at the thought of more food

Brian Well, actually—er—no. I'm—I'm not really very hungry.

Hilary Don't be silly. You must be ravenous. And it's delicious. You won't be able to resist it.

Brian Won't I?

Hilary *Coq au vin.*

Brian considers in pained silence

Brian I beg your pardon?

Hilary That's what we're having.

Brian (*appalled*) *Coq au vin?*
Hilary You don't like it.
Brian Yes, I do. I love it. Really. Love it.
Hilary Oh, good! I'll go and get you a nice *big* helping!

She goes out into the kitchen

Brian looks miserable and apprehensive. The Lights fade up in the other flat

George and Jessica are sitting on the sofa

Jessica Darling?
George H'm?
Jessica I really don't think you ought to leave the spare key under the geraniums.

George hesitates, uncertainly

George Sorry?
Jessica Outside the front door. I mean—*any*body could find it.
George The spare key?
Jessica Yes. And then they could wander in here—and do ... whatever they wanted to do.
George Pinch the silver?
Jessica Amongst other things. They could come in here. And cook meals. Use the place to dry their wet clothes and so on.
George I don't think anybody would do that, would they?
Jessica You never know. Entertain nurses. Anything.
George Good Lord...

He is puzzled, unsure how Jessica knows about the key

In the other flat, Hilary returns with a tray on which is a plate of coq au vin, a knife and fork and a table napkin

Hilary Here we are! You'll feel much better for this.
Brian Will I?

She puts the tray on his knee and fastens a napkin around his neck

Hilary There! Doesn't that look delicious?

He surveys it without enthusiasm

Brian Yes—lovely...

In the other flat, Jessica finishes her drink and gets up

Jessica Well, come on—drink up!
George What?
Jessica Darling, it's time for bed.
George Is it?
Jessica I thought you were so keen to go to bed.
George Well, I suppose I was—in a way.
Jessica In a way? Darling, I've been in America for two weeks!
George Yes. I know, and I've missed you very much. But I am a bit
   hungry.
Jessica (*highly insulted*) Hungry?!

In the other flat...

Hilary Well, I think I'll go to bed.
Brian Oh?
Hilary You don't mind, do you, darling? I don't want to put you off your
   food. And I am rather tired.
Brian Oh. Right.

In the other flat...

Jessica (*steaming*) Hungry? Didn't you get anything, then?
George No, nothing at all! I was too late...
Jessica Well, we mustn't let you go *hungry*, must we? (*She sets off,
   frostily, to get her suitcase*)

In the other flat...

Hilary Good-night, darling. (*She gives Brian a quick kiss and starts to go*)
Brian I won't be very long——
Hilary Oh, don't you hurry, darling. I want you to enjoy your *coq au vin*.

In the other flat...

Jessica is going with her case

George Where are you going?
Jessica (*fed up*) I'm going to bed! Good-night, George. You'll find some
    coq au vin in the kitchen!

In the other flat...

Hilary (*waving her finger at Brian, playfully*) And don't you come to bed
    until you've eaten every bit of it.

Brian gazes mournfully at his coq au vin

*The ladies start to go, then both turn back in unison to look at their
respective husbands: Jessica glaring at George, Hilary smiling at Brian*

Jessica ⎫
              (*together*) Enjoy your meal!
Hilary ⎭

    The ladies go off to their bedrooms

*A pause. Both men sitting in silence. Then they get up in unison and set off
for their kitchens, Brian carrying his tray of unwanted* coq au vin. *They
disappear. A short pause, then they both re-appear. Brian no longer has
his tray. George now has a tray on which is a plate of* coq au vin. *They both
look pleased with themselves*

*George sits down with his food, unfolds his table napkin, uses the pepper
and salt, etc., while Brian goes to his sofa and finishes off Hilary's glass
of wine. He is about to go to bed when he notices something. He returns
slowly, peering at what he has seen. He sits on the sofa and picks up
George's bicycle clips from the table. He has one bicycle clip in each hand
and looks from one to the other, puzzled. In the other flat, George is facing
his food, happily and enthusiastically*

Brian (*grimly*) Now what's *this*?
George (*smiling*) *Coq au vin*!

Black-out

ACT II

The same. The next morning. The theme music plays

The Lights come up in Brian and Hilary's flat. Brian is dressed for work. He is preparing to go, putting papers, etc., into his briefcase

Hilary comes in from the bedroom. She is wearing a delightful dressing-gown and is a little sleepy. The music fades

Hilary Good-morning, darling...
Brian (*grunting*) Morning.
Hilary You sound a little grumpy.
Brian (*grumpily*) I'm all right.
Hilary I had a wonderful night.
Brian (*abruptly*) Oh, did you really?
Hilary Yes. I was fast asleep before you came to bed. (*She pours herself some coffee*) Did you enjoy the *coq au vin*?

Brian reacts, guiltily

Brian Er—yes. Lovely. Very nice.
Hilary Did you finish all of it like I told you?
Brian Er ... most of it, yes.
Hilary Good. (*Brightly*) Just off to work, darling?

He looks at her, irritably

Brian I usually go to work on a Thursday. It's Saturday and Sunday I stay at home
Hilary Is it only Thursday?
Brian Well, it was Wednesday yesterday.
Hilary (*dreamily*) Good Lord...!
Brian Are you feeling all right?
Hilary Yes, darling. Wonderful. Will you be jogging again tonight?

Brian Wednesday's my jogging night.
Hilary You could go again.
Brian Two nights running?
Hilary Why not?
Brian I don't think I could manage it two nights running.
Hilary I mean—don't feel you have to stay in just because of me. (*She settles down on the sofa with her coffee*)

Brian looks at her suspiciously

Brian You seem very keen to get rid of me.
Hilary I just thought you might secretly *want* to do it again tonight and be staying in just for me.
Brian Oh. No.
Hilary That's all right, then. Because… *I* may go out for a while.
Brian (*surprised*) Jogging?
Hilary (*laughing*) No!
Brian Where?
Hilary (*airily*) I may go out for a couple of hours. To meet a friend.
Brian (*coldly*) I see. Anyone I know?
Hilary N-no… I don't think you've met.

Brian moves to her, importantly

Brian This hasn't got anything to do with bicycle clips, has it?

She looks up from her coffee, blankly

Hilary I beg your pardon?
Brian You're not a secret cyclist, by any chance, are you?
Hilary Darling, what *are* you talking about?
Brian You haven't taken to riding a bicycle?
Hilary (*sleepily bemused*) No. And even if I had I wouldn't be wearing bicycle clips. Not with a skirt.
Brian (*heavily*) That's what I thought.

With great moment he produces George's bicycle clips from his pocket

There! What do you think of those?

Hilary views them impassively

Hilary I suppose they're *quite* nice. As bicycle clips go. I'm not much of an authority. I'm not really into bicycle clips. Where did you get them?

Brian (*exploding*) I found them! Here! On the table! There! (*He plonks them down on the table in front of her*)

She is transfixed for a moment, gazing at the bicycle clips, then she thinks of a way out

Hilary Ah! So *that's* where they'd got to?

Brian What?

Hilary I've been looking for them everywhere.

Brian Frightened I might see them, eh?

Hilary Why should I be frightened you'd see them?

Brian Well, let's face it—(*with heavy innuendo*) they're *men's* bicycle clips, aren't they?

Hilary Is there a *difference*? I would have thought that bicycle clips were fairly sexless.

Brian (*grimly*) I think *I* know the answer...!

Hilary To sexless bicycle clips?

Brian You may as well tell me! Who do they belong to?

A tense pause, then...

Hilary (*serenely*) Well—to the window-cleaner, of course.

He looks at her stonily for a moment

Brian Window-cleaner?

Hilary Yes. He came in with his bucket to get some water.

Brian In his bicycle clips?

Hilary Well, he can't afford a car.

Brian I'm very surprised, the prices *he* charges! Why the hell did he take his bicycle clips off?

Hilary *I* don't know, darling. I didn't ask him. It's not the sort of question you ask a window-cleaner with a bucketful of water. Perhaps they were too tight. Cutting off the blood supply to his feet.

Brian You mean—he just came in here with his bucket and took off his bicycle clips? Without so much as by-your-leave?

Hilary I suppose he must have done, yes.

Brian Why couldn't he put them in his pocket?

Hilary I expect he thought they'd weigh him down when he started to go up his ladder.

Brian Well, why didn't you give them to him when he left?

Hilary (*getting irritated*) Because until he'd gone I didn't know he'd left them, did I? You're asking a lot of questions. They belonged to the window-cleaner. All right?

Brian is grudgingly satisfied

Brian Yes. All right. Fine. Good. (*He picks up his briefcase and umbrella, ready to go*)

Hilary Who on earth did you *think* they belonged to?

Brian returns, a trifle shamefaced

Brian Well ... you'll never believe this ... but I thought—(*he chuckles*) I thought perhaps you'd got a lover.

Hilary A lover in bicycle clips?

Brian (*laughing*) Yes, I know! It's ridiculous, isn't it?

Hilary Why?

Brian What?

Hilary Why is it ridiculous that I should have a lover?

Brian Well ... you're not like that.

Hilary Why not?

Brian What?

Hilary Why shouldn't I be like that?

Brian Because—because you wouldn't do a thing like that. Not to *me*.

Hilary Why not?

Brian (*getting flustered*) Because I'm your husband!

Hilary Oh, I see. Well, I wouldn't bank on it.

Brian What?

Hilary For all *you* know, when *you're* puffing and panting around the park, I might be puffing and panting around here. (*She smiles at him, enigmatically*)

Brian is not sure whether she is joking or not. Optimistically, he opts for the negative and grins at her

Brian Aah! You're pulling my leg!

Hilary Probably. You'll never be certain, though, will you?
Brian Of course I'm certain.
Hilary (*serenely*) I'm very glad to hear it. So stop going on about bicycle clips and window-cleaners. I'm sure I'm just as faithful to you as you are to me.

Brian reacts to this with some embarrassment

Brian Ah. Yes. Of course you are! Right. (*He looks at his watch*) Good heavens! I'd better go, or I'll be late. Goodbye, darling. I'll—I'll see you tonight. (*He opens the front door*)

Hilary smiles into her coffee cup

Hilary I'll try not to be *too* late.
Brian What? Oh. Yes. Right.

> *Brian backs out, nervously, almost falling over his briefcase as he goes, and closes the door behind him*

Hilary watches him go, smiling at his discomfort. But the moment he has gone, she leaps up, collects the bicycle clips and runs to the mobile telephone. She dials a number

The Lights come up in George and Jessica's flat. The telephone is ringing

> *Jessica comes down the stairs and lifts the receiver. She is wearing an apron (the one Wendy wore)*

Jessica Hullo?

Hilary hesitates, not wanting to speak to Jessica

Hilary Ah ... er...
Jessica (*puzzled*) What?
Hilary Er ... h'm...
Jessica Hullo? Who is that?
Hilary Aaaaa...!

> *Hilary hangs up in panic and runs out into the bedroom as the Lights fade in her flat*

Jessica hangs up, looking bewildered

George comes in from the kitchen with a cup of coffee. He is dressed in a rather loud sports jacket, trousers and a heavy pair of golfing shoes

George Who was that?

Jessica Some idiot doing heavy breathing.

George At this time of the morning?

Jessica Did you finish off the *coq au vin* last night?

George Yes—rather! I—er—I'm sorry about ... well—you know.

Jessica Don't apologise. You can't help being hungry. But I can remember the days when you thought that sex was more interesting than stew. (*She notices his clothes*) You're not going to work dressed like that, are you?

George looks down at his jacket

George What's wrong with it?

Jessica You usually go to work in your blue suit.

George Ah—yes. I seem to have mislaid it.

Jessica *Mislaid* it?

George Yes. I must have sent it to the cleaners.

Jessica peers at his shoes without enthusiasm

Jessica I don't much care for those shoes, either. Hardly the thing for the office. More at home on the links.

George Links?

Jessica Golf links.

George Cobblers.

Jessica What?

George I sent them to the cobbler's. They're being mended.

Jessica Good heavens. I go away for two weeks and your wardrobe becomes a disaster area.

George (*a little hurt*) I thought this jacket was rather nice...

Jessica makes up her mind to speak about Brian and Wendy, and moves to him purposefully

He eyes her warily

Jessica George…
George Yes?
Jessica There's something I think you ought to know. Something that *I* know about last night.

George reacts nervously and hastily finishes his coffee

George Well, I haven't got a lot of time——
Jessica (*firmly*) You've time for this.
George Have I?
Jessica You don't want to get to work too early. Not in *those* shoes.
George Oh. Right.
Jessica I should sit down if I were you.
George Is it as bad as all that?
Jessica Very possibly. What I have to tell you may come as a shock.
George Ah. Then I *will* sit down.

He sits down and crosses his legs, but realizes this makes his unpopular shoes more noticeable and hastily uncrosses them and tries to hide his shoes behind his legs

Jessica It's all a question of geraniums.
George (*remembering*) Ah! You mentioned geraniums last night.
Jessica Exactly. And when I woke up this morning I had time to think about them fully. I wasn't going to tell you, but I think you should know and take whatever action you think suitable.
George About the geraniums?
Jessica About what lies *under* the geraniums.

He thinks, then remembers

George Ah!
Jessica Precisely.
George The spare key?
Jessica Exactly. I came back here last night—and what do you think I found?
George Under the geraniums?
Jessica In here!

George attempts to escape

George (*stammering*) I—I—I—I really must get off to work!

She pushes him heavily back into his seat

Jessica Now! Where do you think Brian was last night?

George Ah—let's see now. Yesterday was Wednesday. So Brian was on the trot. Jogging around the park.

Jessica He may have started by jogging around the park, but he ended up in here. He used the key from beneath the geraniums to get in here—with a girl!

George overdoes his disbelief at such an idea

George Brian? With a girl? I don't believe it.

Jessica He said she was a nurse. From the Red Cross.

George's inspiration does not fail him

George Oh—*that* girl!

Jessica looks at him, slightly out of her stride

Jessica What?

George Well, I didn't know you meant *that* girl.

Jessica (*surprised*) You mean you know about her?

George Of course I know about her. She's a very dedicated young lady, I can tell you.

Jessica (*coldly*) Oh, *is* she?

George Oh, yes. You see—how can I put this?—well, Brian's reached the age, which all of us get to sooner or later, when jogging—or any other violent physical exertion—cannot be taken too lightly. You see? This is probably giving away a secret, but Brian's health is not all it might be. (*He taps his chest sympathetically*) Dicky heart. So Brian—who, whatever else you may say about him, is a man fully aware of his responsibilities as a husband and as a member of society—realizes that when he goes jogging, he must never go without a fully-trained nurse in attendance.

Jessica gazes at him in astonishment

Jessica You mean *she* trots around *with* him?

George Well ... not *all* the time. But she's always ... within reach.

Jessica Yes, I bet she is!

George Poor Brian. He must have been so embarrassed when you came in and found him.

Jessica Yes. He was.

George I mean, imagine what *he* thought that *you* thought. And I expect you did.

Jessica Yes, I did!

George There you are, then.

Jessica Perhaps he should give up jogging.

George He has considered it.

Jessica Really?

George Oh, yes. Many times. But a man like Brian doesn't give up something like that very easily. He just likes to keep at it. In spite of everything. In spite of the risk. Keeps at it. Last night, presumably he was taken ill while he was at it—jogging—and needed immediate attention.

Jessica He tripped under an oak tree and fell in a pond!

George Ah—that's what he told you. He wouldn't want you to know the truth, now would he? A man has his pride.

Jessica You mean she ... she really *is* a nurse?

George Oh, yes. Shortish?

Jessica Yes.

George Blonde-ish?

Jessica Yes.

George Blue eye-ish?

Jessica Yes.

George Er—(*he mimes a bosom*) -ish?

Jessica Yes!

George That's her!

Jessica She wasn't dressed like a nurse.

George Well, of course not. That would give the game away, wouldn't it? (*He looks at his watch*) Good Lord! Is that the time? I really must go! (*He puts his coffee cup down and gets up*)

Jessica (*remorsefully*) I feel awful now. I'd no idea...

George And you still wouldn't have any idea if you hadn't come home early and caught them. (*He corrects himself quickly*) Found them!

Jessica You didn't mind my telling you about it?

George (*generously*) Of course not, darling.

Jessica I just felt you ought to know.

George And now *you* know why I leave *what* I leave under the geraniums.
Jessica In case of emergency.
George Precisely. Goodbye, darling. (*He kisses her lightly*) I'll see you tonight.
Jessica Yes.

George casts a grateful look heavenwards and heads for the front door. He hesitates for a moment

George Oh, and darling——
Jessica Yes?
George You won't tell Hilary anything about this, will you? Brian wouldn't want her to know that he needed nursing.

He smiles in a world-weary way, and goes, closing the door behind him

Jessica looks thoughtful, then collects his coffee cup and goes into the kitchen as the Lights fade. The theme music comes in

The Lights come up in the other flat

Hilary is coming out of the bedroom with an armful of towels. She goes to the chest, puts down the towels and opens the lid to put the towels inside. She reacts in horror at what she sees. She lifts out George's suit and shoes and looks at them, realizing that he must have gone home with no clothes on. She runs out to the kitchen and returns with a carrier bag. She puts the suit and shoes into the carrier bag, puts the towels into the chest and closes the lid. She picks up the carrier bag containing George's clothes and starts to go out to the bedroom

The Lights fade out in her flat

The Lights come up in George and Jessica's flat. The music fades

The doorbell rings

Jessica comes in and goes to answer it. She opens the door. Brian is there with his umbrella and briefcase. Jessica is surprised

Jessica Oh, it's you!

Brian Has George gone to work?

Jessica Yes.

Brian Oh, good. (*He walks into the room*)

Jessica (*following him*) Mind you, you wouldn't have thought he was going to work if you'd seen the clothes he was wearing.

Brian Well, at least he was *wearing* some clothes!

Jessica Sorry?

Brian Never mind. (*He puts his umbrella and briefcase down on the padded seat*)

Jessica He looks just like a bookie. Did you want to see him?

Brian No. I wanted to see *you*.

Jessica Oh, I *am* flattered. (*Then she goes to him anxiously*) Brian, you seem a little breathless. Do you think you ought to sit down? Put your feet up?

Brian What?

Jessica Rest for a while?

Brian does not know what she is talking about

Brian Well, I've only been up an hour and a half. I don't usually begin to tire until teatime.

Jessica Oh, good! Can I get you a cup of coffee, then? Or is caffeine bad for you?

Brian (*puzzled*) Er—no. No, I can handle caffeine. A cup of coffee would be nice. (*He goes to the sofa*)

Jessica Fine. Sugar?

Brian No, thanks.

Jessica Very wise.

She goes out to the kitchen

He sits, bewildered by her behaviour

She returns with a cup of coffee and takes it to him

Here we are!

Brian Thanks. (*He takes a sip of his coffee, then looks at her, a little uncertainly*) You ... you can probably guess why I'm here.

Jessica Er—not really, no.

Brian (*sheepishly*) Well, it's—it's about ... last night.

Jessica Last night?

Brian Yes. You coming home and ... and finding me and—er——

Jessica Wendy?

Brian Yes.

Jessica Well, it was a surprise certainly, Brian. You see, I didn't know anything about it.

Brian How could you? I knew George would never tell you. He's a good friend. He knows how to keep a secret. And if you hadn't come home early, you wouldn't have found us.

Jessica (*generously*) You mustn't worry about that.

Brian Oh, good! I mean, the story I told you last night about the oak tree and the pond and all that—well, I could hardly expect you to believe that, could I?

Jessica (*smiling*) Well, it was a bit far-fetched, wasn't it? But honestly you don't have to worry.

Brian Don't I?

Jessica You see, as a matter of fact, I do know the truth. (*She sits beside him*)

Brian gazes at her in surprise

Brian Y-y-you do?

Jessica Oh, yes. George told me all about it.

Brian (*appalled*) George *told* you?

Jessica Yes.

Brian The rotten devil!

Jessica No, no—you mustn't blame George. He did the right thing.

Brian He did?

Jessica Yes, of course. I'd have known about it eventually, anyway. (*Sadly*) I mean, presumably we *all* will...

Brian Not if *I* can help it! (*He grins*)

Jessica Well, that's very brave of you, Brian. Very brave. But you really shouldn't keep something like this to yourself. It's far better to talk about it. Have it out in the open.

He stares at her in astonishment

Brian Have it out in the open?

Jessica Yes, of course.

Brian (*bemused*) Funny, I hadn't looked at it quite like that. And that's really why I popped in on my way to work. You see, I—er—I don't really want Hilary to know about it. So I'd be grateful if—well, if you wouldn't mind keeping shtum. You see, Hilary might misunderstand the situation. Oh, I feel awful asking you. You being a friend of Hilary's and all that. But let's face it, these things do happen and—well, you're a man of the world, Jessica—and you know as well as I do that such things aren't really important between a man and a woman, not when you really get down to it; and I wouldn't want Hilary to be upset by it.

Jessica is watching him with increasing admiration

Jessica Of course you wouldn't, Brian. And I think it's very considerate of you.
Brian (*surprised*) You—you do?
Jessica Of course. And you really—honestly—don't want Hilary to find out?
Brian Well ... no. I think it better not.
Jessica (*putting a hand on his arm*) I must say Brian—I admire you.

For the life of him, Brian cannot understand why

Brian Do you? Really? Good Lord...
Jessica And if you don't want Hilary to know about it—(*she pats his arm*) you can rely on me to keep it a secret. I wouldn't *dream* of telling her.
Brian (*gratefully*) Thanks, Jessica. I knew I could rely on your discretion. (*He puts his cup down, relieved*) Well, that was much easier than I expected. I was shaking with nerves when I got here, I can tell you!
Jessica Poor Brian... I quite understand. (*Suddenly*) I've got a great idea! You won't be jogging again tonight, will you?
Brian No. I—(*he nudges her playfully*) I only "jog" on Wednesdays! (*He laughs*)

Jessica is a little puzzled by this, but dismisses it

Jessica Yes, well, I think you're very wise. It might be too much of a strain if you did it more than once a week.

Brian roars with laughter at this, and then pretends to be shocked

Brian Oooh, Jessica! You're really very wicked, you know. I suppose this sort of thing happens a lot in America and Holland and all those other places you go to?

Jessica is naturally rather puzzled by his mirth

Jessica Well, a fair amount, yes. But, I must say, they usually tell their wives about it.
Brian (*astonished*) Tell their wives?
Jessica Oh, yes. Then their wives can be on hand in case they have a heart attack.
Brian Good Lord...! That's a very modern attitude. I can understand the Dutch being like that, but the Americans—well! I *am* surprised.
Jessica Anyway, as tonight you won't be doing any——
Jessica ⎫
Brian ⎭ (*together*) Jogging!

Brian laughs

Jessica I thought, as I've just got back from the States, you and Hilary might like to come to dinner.
Brian (*considering*) Wouldn't you find that a bit embarrassing? Now that you know about me.
Jessica Of course not. We're all still the same people, aren't we?
Brian (*impressed*) My God, Jessica, I do respect you. Really respect you. (*He grins*) You're a bit of a male chauvinist pig, aren't you? (*He roars with laughter again*)

Jessica proceeds, in spite of her puzzlement

Jessica So ... so you will come to dinner tonight?
Brian Love to!
Jessica Good. That's settled, then. (*She leans forward, confidentially*) And you don't have to worry about anything. I studied nursing for two years (*She takes his coffee cup to the crescent table*)
Brian Nursing?

She gives a gesture of secrecy

Jessica 'nough said!

Brian (*doubtfully*) Oh. Yes... (*He collects his briefcase and umbrella and starts to go*) I'd better be off or I'll be late for work. (*He stops, suddenly remembering something*) Heavens! I've just remembered Hilary said she was going out tonight.
Jessica Oh. Oh, dear. What a pity. But *you* can still come?
Brian Oh, yes.
Jessica Good. About seven-thirty?
Brian On the dot.

He starts to go again

Jessica I tell you what—as Hilary can't be here, why don't you bring Wendy?

Brian drops his briefcase and umbrella. He cannot believe his ears

Brian Bring Wendy?
Jessica Why not?
Brian Bring Wendy here to dinner with you and George?
Jessica Well, you said Hilary couldn't come.
Brian Yes, I know, but——
Jessica Then bring Wendy.

Brian smiles nervously

Brian I'd ... I'd feel a bit embarrassed.
Jessica There's no need to feel embarrassed. I mean, the three of us would all know why Wendy was here.
Brian Exactly! That's what I mean! I'd be embarrassed.
Jessica I don't see what's so embarrassing about it. After all, under the circumstances Wendy *ought* to be here, in case you suddenly wanted to lie down for a bit.

Brian gazes at her, a stranger to such tolerance

Brian Well ... I'm not sure, Jessica. I know you're a pretty understanding woman. Fantastically so. But I don't think old George would approve.
Jessica It was old George who put the key under the geraniums, remember. You leave old George to me. He'll approve all right.

Brian begins to bend to pick up his briefcase and umbrella, but Jessica
(considering his dicky heart) stops him and picks them up for him

   Bring Wendy.
Brian No—no, I couldn't—really. It's kind, but I couldn't. Honestly.
Jessica Well, I think you're making a great big fuss over nothing.
Brian Yes, I know you do, and I can't understand it...!
Jessica All right, then. It's up to you. But if you change your mind, Wendy
   will be very welcome.
Brian Thanks. I'll see you tonight, then.
Jessica We'll be waiting!
Brian And thank you again, Jessica. (*He gives the thumbs-up sign*)
   You're a pal!

   He goes out, elated but bewildered

Jessica sighs, pleased with her philanthropy, picks up his coffee cup and
heads for the kitchen

The Lights fade in her flat

The Lights come up in the other flat

The doorbell is ringing

   Hilary comes in from the bedroom and goes to open the door

   George is there in his bright jacket

Hilary Good heavens! You're off to the races!

George plods in and tries to be patient

George I am *not* off to the races.
Hilary (*delightedly*) Ah! You've taken a day off work and come back to
   carry on from where we left off?
George Oh, no! No. I couldn't face *coq au vin* at this time of the morning.
Hilary I wasn't meaning *coq au vin*. I say, this *is* a lovely surprise! What
   a good thing I didn't get dressed.

She takes his hand and starts to lead him towards the bedroom. He resists

George Where are we going?
Hilary Don't be silly, darling. You know where the bedroom is.
George I didn't come here for that!
Hilary Then what *did* you come here for?
George I left something behind.
Hilary Ah—yes. I know. I telephoned you this morning, but Jessica answered.
George So it was you?
Hilary What?
George The heavy breather. For heaven's sake, why didn't you *say* something?
Hilary I could hardly tell Jessica that you left your bicycle clips here, could I?
George Bicycle clips?

Hilary picks up the bicycle clips from the telephone table

Hilary Brian found them over there on the table.
George (*alarmed*) What?!
Hilary Don't worry. I told him they belonged to the window-cleaner.
George He didn't find the clothes I left behind, as well, did he?
Hilary Fortunately not. Why on earth didn't you take your suit and shoes with you last night?
George Because I couldn't find them. I left them over there. Neat and tidy. Where the hell did you put them?
Hilary I put them in the chest, of course.
George It was no time for playing hunt the slipper!
Hilary Your wife was here and she might have wondered what your clothes were doing in my flat.
George Ah—yes, of course.

Hilary goes into the bedroom

George crosses to the chest and opens it to get his suit. He reacts when he finds it is empty and paces in an agitated circle

Towards the end of the following speech, Hilary returns from the bedroom with the carrier bag of clothes

They're not here! They've gone! He's found them! Oh, my God, he's found them. Brian's found my suit and my shoes. And if you find a man's suit and a man's shoes what the hell are you going to think? I bet I know where he is now! He'll be in the City. He'll have gone to buy a gun. They sell them in the City. He'll be selecting a gun this very minute! Picking one out carefully. A gun. And bullets! And then he'll wait for me to come home tonight and then—my God, he'll shoot me! (*He comes face-to-face with the carrier bag that Hilary has brought in from the bedroom, and stares at it*) What's that?

Hilary (*smiling serenely*) Your suit and shoes, of course.

George You said they were in the... (*indicating the chest*)

Hilary They were. But I put them in the carrier bag.

George In the carrier bag? What were you going to do with them? You weren't going to take them over to my flat, were you?

Hilary I couldn't leave them *here*!

George (*pacing away below the sofa*) Oh, lovely! That would have been lovely. Ring the bell, hand them over to Jessica and say, "These are your husband's clothes. He took them off in my flat and forgot them!" Very nice indeed.

Hilary Don't be silly. Of course I wasn't going to do that. (*A beat*) I thought I'd take them to Oxfam.

George (*gazing at her, appalled*) Oxfam? Hand over my best suit to the Third World?

Hilary I thought it was the safest thing to do. I could hardly leave it here. I had to make a snap decision.

George You certainly did that! This is a good suit. They'd have put it in the window.

Hilary (*pleased*) Oh, that would have been nice.

George Oh, yes. Then Jessica might have walked past the shop and gone in and bought it back for fifty p!

Hilary Well, at least you'd have got it back.

George (*thoughtfully*) I never realized that adultery needed such strong nerves.

He takes off his trousers. Hilary smiles delightedly

Hilary Oh, good! You've changed your mind.

She hastens across to Brian's photograph and puts it face down again. George sees this, runs across and stands it up again

George Don't be ridiculous! I'm going to change into my suit and then
    go to work.
Hilary Oh. What a shame…

*George proceeds to fold up his trousers neatly, standing in his jacket and
shirt. Hilary is deep in thought*

    George…?
George (*busy with his trousers*) Yes?
Hilary If you left your suit *here* last night—how did you get home?
George On my bicycle, of course.
Hilary In your shirt and socks and no bicycle clips?
George I didn't have much choice, did I? It caused quite a stir, I can tell
    you.
Hilary (*laughing*) Yes. I bet it did!

George starts to take off his jacket

    I wish I'd seen you bicycling along in your shirt and pants!
George Don't be daft. I had a dressing-gown on.

He freezes, remembering, the jacket half on

Hilary What's the matter?
George I had a dressing-gown on…!
Hilary Oh, good.
George No, not good. (*Bleakly*) It was Brian's dressing-gown.

They look at each other in horror

Hilary Oh, my God! And where is it now?
George It's in my flat! Under the sofa!

The doorbell rings. George stands there miserably in his shirt and socks

    Oh, God—here I go again…!

*He puts the bicycle clips on to his bare shins and plods wearily out into
the bedroom*

Hilary hastily gathers up George's discarded clothes

Brian (*off*) Hilary! Are you there?
Hilary (*calling*) Coming, darling! Just a minute!

She opens a cupboard, shoves the clothes inside and closes the door. Then she goes to open the front door

Brian comes in quickly

Brian I left my key behind. I remembered you said you were going out tonight, so I had to come back and get it. (*He notices her state of undress*) Good heavens, you've been back to bed again.
Hilary No. He didn't want to.
Brian What?
Hilary (*quickly*) I didn't want to! I'd had enough sleep. Far too much.
Brian I should jolly well think so. You're not staying like that all day, are you? (*He laughs, playfully*) Or are you expecting the window-cleaner to call again?
Hilary He's already been.
Brian Has he really? Dirty devil. (*He laughs, looking about for his key*)
Hilary He came to get his bicycle clips.
Brian A likely tale! I must have left my key in the kitchen. Any coffee going? I may as well have a cup while I'm here.
Hilary Yes. (*Raising her voice for George's benefit*) Let's go into the kitchen and I'll make you some fresh. (*She picks up the coffee pot and pulls Brian out into the kitchen*)

George comes out of the bedroom and tiptoes across to where he left his clothes. He reacts in alarm when he sees they have gone; then smiles, remembering the chest. He goes to it confidently and lifts the lid. He cannot believe that his clothes are not there

Brian (*off*) Well, it's not in here. I'll have another look in the sitting-room.

George looks about in panic. Then he remembers the leopard skin on the wall. He races across and drapes himself against it as he did before

Brian walks in from the kitchen and looks about for his key, not seeing George

George suddenly realizes that he is not wearing the matching dressing-gown this time, thereby destroying his camouflage. He goes quickly to the front door, opens it and, for the second time in twenty-four hours, runs out in his shirt and socks

Brian turns when he hears the door close, looks puzzled and goes to the front door. He opens it and looks out

Hilary...?

Hilary looks out of the kitchen

Hilary Brian!

She holds up his latchkey with a big smile. Puzzled, Brian follows her back into the kitchen as—

The Lights fade

Music plays as the Lights come up in George and Jessica's flat. The same evening

Jessica is coming in from the kitchen with a tray on which are various dishes of nuts, crisps, etc. She is wearing an attractive dinner dress. She goes about, putting the dishes in different places, then goes out to the kitchen again, taking the empty tray with her

George comes in from the front door, rather furtively. He is wearing a nondescript, ill-fitting brown suit that is far too tight and rather short in the leg. Relieved that Jessica is not there, he goes quickly to the sofa and kneels down to look under it

Jessica returns. The music stops. She is rather surprised to see him on all fours in front of the sofa

Jessica George!

He falls on his face. She comes to him, puzzled

What on earth are you doing down there?

George looks up at her

George What?

Jessica You're on your knees in front of the sofa.

George Ah. Yes. I ... I was looking for a cuff-link.

Jessica What?

George A cuff-link. You know what cuff-links are. Well, I was looking
for one. Because I dropped one, you see. On the floor. So I was down
here looking for it.

Jessica (*peering at him*) It doesn't look to me as if you're short of a cuff-
link.

George Doesn't it?

Jessica You only wear two at a time, don't you?

He looks at his cuffs and pretends to be surprised

George Good Lord! They're both there all the time! One on the end of
each little sleeve. See? One, two. Well, well! I could have sworn I heard
something drop.

Jessica (*with a glint*) Well, it wasn't a cuff-link.

George No... (*He gets up and kisses her briefly but enthusiastically*)
Hullo, darling!

She looks a little surprised by his exuberance

Jessica What sort of a day did you have?

George Oh—fairly non-vintage.

Jessica Never mind. We're going to have a nice evening.

George Are we? Oh, good.

*Jessica is looking at him, rather puzzled. He notices her look and shifts
uncomfortably in his ill-fitting suit, tries to pull the jacket down a bit, etc.*

   Why are you staring at me?

Jessica Because you look different.

George I don't expect I've grown much since this morning.

Jessica I don't remember you looking like this when you went off to work.
(*She suddenly realizes*) Ah! I know!

George Do you?

Jessica You were wearing that dreadful jacket. And those awful shoes. That's what it was. What have you done with them?

George Ah. Yes. I—er—I took them off.

Jessica (*surprised*) Took them off?

George Yes.

Jessica Where?

A pause

George (*blankly*) What?

Jessica Where did you take them off?

George Does it matter? You didn't like them. You said so. You said I shouldn't go to work dressed like that. So I took them off.

Jessica What did you do with them?

He looks at her blankly again

George What?

Jessica What did you do with them when you took them off?

George Gave them to Oxfam. I like to help the Third World. So I did a deal with Oxfam. The lady was very pleased. I gave her my jacket and trousers and she gave me this suit. (*He turns around to show it off*) Not bad, eh?

Jessica (*bemused*) Well, it's ... quite nice. But George—you don't usually get your clothes from Oxfam.

George That's very true. But I couldn't very well come back home because *you* were here.

Jessica What?

George (*quickly*) Asleep! I thought you might be asleep. Still feeling a bit jet-lagged—you know? So I didn't want to disturb you.

Jessica That was very thoughtful.

George (*modestly*) Yes. That's what *I* thought. So Oxfam was the next best thing.

Jessica (*puzzled*) But, George—if you were going to change your clothes, why didn't you do it before you left for work?

George Don't be silly, darling. I was late enough already.

Jessica (*persisting*) George!

He changes the subject hastily

George My God! I could do with a drink. (*He plods off to the drinks cupboard*) Can I get something for you?

Jessica Sherry would be nice. (*She sits on the sofa*)

George One sherry coming up.

He notices the dishes of nuts as he goes for the drinks

Are we going in for nuts tonight, then?

Jessica What?

George Seem to be a lot of nuts all over the place.

Jessica Well, we usually have nuts when people come to dinner, don't we?

George Very true. *And* those curly, crispy things that taste of fish. Is that what's happening, then? People coming to dinner.

Jessica Yes. I thought it would be rather nice, as I've been away for a couple of weeks.

George Good idea. Anyone I know?

Jessica Brian.

George Oh, yes. I know him. That'll make a change.

Jessica Well, he *is* one of our oldest friends.

George arrives with a sherry for Jessica and a gin-and-tonic for himself

George Quite right. Here we are.

Jessica Thanks. (*She takes the sherry*) But I'll tell you something very interesting.

George Oh, yes?

Jessica (*importantly*) Hilary can't come.

George No?

Jessica No.

George Ah.

Jessica And do you know why?

George Haven't a clue.

Jessica Because she's made— (*with heavy innuendo*) other arrangements.

George Has she, by Jove? Good for Hilary. What other arrangements?

Jessica Well, *I* don't know, do I?

George I'm very surprised. You usually have your finger on the pulse.

Jessica (*knowingly*) But I've got a pretty good idea!

George I thought you would have. (*He sits beside her*) Cheers, darling!

Jessica Cheers.

George proffers a dish of nuts

George Care for a nut?
Jessica *Now?*
George May as well make a start on them.

They both take nuts and munch away happily

Jessica George...
George H'm?
Jessica How *well* do you know Hilary?

*George chokes on his nuts. He points desperately at his drink. Jessica
passes it to him and he drinks some of it gratefully*

Are you all right, darling?
George Yes. I think so. (*He coughs and splutters a little and begins to
recover*) Oh, dear. I usually handle my nuts better than that. There we
are. I think I'll survive.

Jessica persists with her train of thought

Jessica I'll tell you why I ask.
George (*blankly*) Sorry?
Jessica About Hilary.
George Ah. Yes.
Jessica Because I went round there last night, and Hilary was behaving
in a very strange way. Very ... furtive.
George That *is* surprising. I've never thought of Hilary as a furtive sort
of person.
Jessica Exactly. *I* was surprised, too. Dancing!
George I beg your pardon?
Jessica Demonstrating a Morris dance.
George (*incredulously*) Hilary?
Jessica Yes.
George Good Lord...
Jessica I got this strange feeling that she was hiding something.

George Don't be ridiculous. Whatever would she be hiding?
Jessica Well, *I* think she had a man in there.

George chokes again, and again indicates his drink. Jessica passes it to him and he sips it, gratefully. She waits until he recovers

George I really must stop eating nuts. Better stick to the curly, fishy things from now on.
Jessica I'm sure there was a man there.
George Well, perhaps he was a Morris dancer! Don't be silly, darling. Hilary would never go in for that sort of thing.
Jessica Why not? She's extremely attractive.
George *(dreamily)* Yes, she certainly is... *(He pulls himself together hastily, kneels on the sofa and leans over the back of it, searching for the dressing gown)*
Jessica And perhaps Brian neglects her. These athletic types quite often neglect their wives, you know.
George Do they really? I didn't know that.
Jessica And I'll tell you another thing that made me suspicious. *(She turns and sees George's backside up in the air)* George! Are you paying attention?

George sits down again and holds up a single nut that he has ostensibly discovered on the floor behind the sofa. He eats it, sheepishly

George Yes, of course.
Jessica Hilary was drinking ... dry martinis.
George Was she really? Good Lord...
Jessica And when I came out of her kitchen I swear I heard the front door close.
George Well?
Jessica Well, I bet it was him! Escaping! What a pity I wasn't a second earlier. I very nearly caught him.
George I'm jolly glad you didn't! *(He empties the dish of nuts into his drink and stirs it)*
Jessica What?
George It would have been so embarrassing. For Hilary! *(He starts to drink but finds his glass is full of nuts)* I think I need another drink. *(He escapes to get a fresh drink)*

Jessica is giggling with delight at the prospect of the situation she only narrowly missed

Jessica Oh, I do wish I'd seen him! I'd love to know what kind of a man Hilary would go in for. (*Thoughtfully*) I think she'd probably go for the more solid, heavy, mature, *older* man.
George (*exploding*) She would not!
Jessica (*surprised*) What?
George You've no right to say that! You can't possibly say that. Whoever he is, he's probably not a day over forty! Fully sound of wind and limb!

Jessica looks astonished by his outburst

Jessica You don't have to get so excited about it.
George (*pacing, angrily, with his drink*) Well, I think it's jolly unfair to suppose that poor Hilary has to saddle herself with some decrepit old geriatric! She's an extremely attractive woman, and if she wants to find herself a lover she doesn't have to go searching amongst the dregs! She can have the pick of the bunch!

He stands there, proud and angry. She gazes at him in surprise

Jessica George—whatever's come over you? Have you been drinking all day?
George No, I have not! (*He throws his drink back in one*)
Jessica Well, you seem to be catching up now.

Whereupon he marches off for another snorter

George It's a good thing that Hilary *isn't* coming to dinner tonight. You'd only be staring at her, and giggling, and making fun of her.
Jessica But George, there's no reason for *you* to be so upset about it.

He calms down a little, realizing that perhaps he is going too far and returns with his drink

George I ... I just don't think you should pry into other people's affairs like that.
Jessica I only said she was furtive...

George *And* that she was a secret martini drinker and Morris dancer!
Jessica *And* that a man's clothes were littered all over her flat...
George (*alarmed*) What?
Jessica Oh, yes. And you'll never believe this, but— (*She breaks off*) Oh,
no. I mustn't tell you. You'll only get cross. (*But she cannot resist it*) Oh,
I *must* tell you! When Hilary and I were going to have some *coq au vin*,
I noticed something quite extraordinary. Hilary ... had a man's tie down
the front of her dress!

George wishes he was a million miles away

What do you think of that? What sort of a man would take off his tie and
shove it down a woman's cleavage? How's that for kinky? He's
probably some sort of sex maniac!

The doorbell rings

Ah—that'll be Brian.
George Talking of sex maniacs...

*Jessica goes to the door. George quickly bends down to look under the
sofa. He cannot see the dressing-gown, but is unable to search further with
Jessica there. Jessica opens the door*

Wendy is there. She is naturally surprised to see Jessica there

Wendy Oh... Sorry, I think I——
Jessica Hullo, Wendy! Come on in.
Wendy (*nervously*) It doesn't matter. I'll just go and——
Jessica Don't be silly. Come on in!

*Wendy comes in nervously. She sees George. He is gazing at her,
appalled. Jessica closes the door and moves to Wendy*

I'm so glad you could come after all.
Wendy (*puzzled*) Were you expecting me, then?
Jessica Of course we were expecting you.
George No, we weren't!
Jessica George! Of course we were expecting her. (*To Wendy*) We

weren't sure if you'd be able to make it or not, but we're delighted that
you could. George, pull yourself together and get Wendy a drink.

George (*wildly*) She doesn't want a drink! You don't want a drink, do
you? No, of course you don't! There! You see? She doesn't want a
drink!

Jessica (*to Wendy*) Ah! I suppose you're not allowed to drink when you're
on duty, is that it? Well, don't you worry. Tonight doesn't really count,
and I promise you that George and I won't say anything about it to the
Red Cross.

Wendy looks totally lost

Wendy I'd like a large gin-and-tonic!

Nobody moves

Jessica George! Large gin-and-tonic for Wendy.

George Oh. Yes. Right. (*He plods away to get it, looking sternly at Wendy
as he goes*)

Jessica leads Wendy down to the sofa

Jessica I'm so glad Brian decided to bring you, after all. He did hesitate
about it, but I assured him it would be all right.

Wendy But he already knew I was coming.

Jessica Brian did?

Wendy Yes. I told him I'd come here tonight. But I didn't think you two
were going to be here!

Jessica (*with a gracious smile*) We *live* here, Wendy.

Wendy Yes, but I assumed you'd be going out. (*She sits on the sofa*)

Jessica (*as to a child*) We can't be going out, Wendy. We're giving a
dinner party. Brian's coming. And I told him I thought it would be a
good idea if he brought you along. (*She sits beside Wendy*) Didn't he
telephone you?

Wendy No...

Jessica Oh, poor Brian. He's so sensitive. You see, he thought that George
wouldn't approve.

Wendy Why not? He always has before.

George intervenes hastily with gin-and-tonic

George Gin-and-tonic!

Wendy Oh—thanks. (*She takes it*)

Jessica It was a good thing you turned up, then, wasn't it? It was a good thing she turned up, then, wasn't—?

George has disappeared behind the sofa again

George!

He re-appears over the back of the sofa

Do pay attention. (*She turns to Wendy again*) Fancy Brian not inviting you. He is a silly boy. Never mind. He'll have a lovely surprise when he finds you here.

George, still searching for his dressing-gown, is on all fours at the end of the sofa, close to being tangled up with Wendy's legs

George...!

George Yes?

Jessica Come on. I'm sure Wendy's dying for some nuts.

George proffers a dish of nuts from his position at the end of the sofa

George Nuts!

Wendy (*jumping*) What?

George Or perhaps you prefer the curly, fishy things?

Wendy Oh. No. No—nuts will be fine. (*She takes some*) Thanks.

Jessica George, aren't you going to change?

George Why?

Jessica I hope you don't intend to eat in an Oxfam suit.

George It's a perfectly good suit.

Wendy Yes. He's better dressed than last time I saw him. (*She grins at George*)

George Nuts! (*He thrusts the dish of nuts at her*)

Jessica (*puzzled*) Oh? What was he wearing last time?

Wendy Not very much! (*She giggles*)

George Nuts! (*He thrusts the nuts at her again*)

Jessica George, I do think you should change. I'm not awfully fond of that suit.

George (*reluctantly*) Oh. All right. (*He gets up*) But I shan't be very long.
Jessica Don't hurry. I'm sure Wendy and I can find lots of things to talk
  about.

George goes off upstairs, in a cloud of apprehension

Jessica turns easily to Wendy

  I must say, Wendy, I think it's wonderful for Brian to have someone like
  you to call on from time to time. You should be very proud of yourself.
  What you're doing for Brian is first class. I thoroughly approve.
Wendy (*puzzled*) Yes, you *do*, don't you? And it's a bit of a surprise.
Jessica Why should it be a surprise? If Brian needs you, and if what you
  do for him is *good* for him, then it's all right with me.

Wendy cannot believe her ears, and takes a big swig of her gin

  Of course I did ask Hilary tonight.
Wendy Hilary?
Jessica Brian's wife.
Wendy (*appalled*) You asked his *wife*?
Jessica Yes, of course. But she couldn't come.
Wendy Thank God for that...! I mean, what would she say if she saw
  me here?
Jessica Oh, I'm sure she'd understand the situation. After all, she's very
  fond of Brian and I know she'd be grateful for anything you can do for
  him.
Wendy I wouldn't take a bet on it.

The doorbell goes

Jessica Ah! That'll be him now!

Jessica goes and opens the front door

  *Brian is there with his briefcase and umbrella. He thrusts a bunch of
  flowers under Jessica's nose*

Brian I brought you some flowers.

Jessica Oh, thank you, Brian. That is kind. (*She takes the flowers and closes the door*)

Brian walks into the room and crosses to the seat below the kitchen door, nodding to Wendy as he passes, but not apparently recognizing her. He puts his briefcase and umbrella down and then reacts to what he has seen. He turns and gazes at Wendy in horror

Brian What the hell are *you* doing here?

Jessica moves between them and smiles contentedly at Wendy

Jessica You see, Wendy? I told you it would be a nice surprise, didn't I? (*To Brian*) You're very naughty. I told you to invite Wendy and you didn't. But she turned up anyway, so serve you right. Will you excuse me a minute? I'll just put these flowers in water. Thank you, Brian. They're really lovely!

She sweeps out to the kitchen

Brian goes desperately to Wendy

Brian You're not supposed to come here tonight!
Wendy Why not? I told you I would.
Brian Yes, but I didn't think you meant it.
Wendy Of course I meant it. I thought you'd have fixed it up with George. Imagine how I felt when I arrived, looking for you, and found other people here.
Brian Other people? They *live* here!
Wendy (*a little hurt*) Well, you should have arranged it like I said.
Brian I can't arrange something like that in five minutes. These things take time.
Wendy It doesn't matter, anyhow. Jessica knows all about us and she doesn't mind at all.
Brian (*puzzled*) Yes. I know. And I can't understand it...
Wendy She told you, then?
Brian Yes, she told *me*, but I didn't think she'd told *you*...
Wendy (*proudly*) She said that what I was doing for you was first class.

He laughs and paces away from her

Brian Yes, it is! But I don't know how *she* knew that.

Wendy And she said that if what I do for you is good for you, then it's all right with her!

Brian Good heavens—Jessica really has become remarkably philanthropic. I expect it's all that foreign travel.

Wendy So we don't have to worry, do we? We can relax and have a nice dinner party.

Brian (*not too keen*) Well, I suppose so...

Wendy And then afterwards——

Brian Afterwards? There won't *be* any afterwards!

Wendy You could persuade them to take the dog for a walk.

Brian They haven't got a dog!

Wendy (*disappointed*) You mean this is going to be *another* night with food and nothing else?

Brian I don't think this dinner party's a good idea. It's going to be so embarrassing...

George comes in from the bedroom. He is now wearing trousers, a shirt and cardigan. He goes briskly to Wendy

George Wendy! You'll have to go!

Wendy Don't be silly. I've still got my gin.

Brian (*smiling politely*) Good evening, George.

George (*glancing at him briefly*) Good evening. (*To Wendy*) You'll have to finish it off and go.

Wendy But I'm invited! Brian—tell him I'm invited.

Brian She's invited.

George She can't stay here. Not under these circumstances. Wednesday nights are one thing, but Thursdays are out of the question.

Brian But Jessica invited her.

George (*wildly*) Jessica doesn't know what's going on!

Brian Of course she does. She's delighted. She said so.

Wendy To both of us.

Brian And you don't have to worry. Hilary can't come.

Wendy It wouldn't matter if she did.

George (*surprised*) What?

Wendy She'd be grateful for anything I can do for Brian.

George (*incredulously*) Have you gone mad?

Wendy Well, that's what Jessica said.

George Jessica is suffering from jet-lag!

Brian George, you need a drink.
George Yes, I know!
Brian (*to Wendy*) Get George a drink.
George (*to Wendy*) Get George a drink.
Wendy Right.
George Whisky.
Brian (*to Wendy*) Whisky.
Wendy Right. (*She goes to get George a whisky*)

Brian takes George aside, confidentially

Brian Look, George—I know this is embarrassing for you. It's embarrassing for me, too. But Jessica knows all about me and Wendy, and she really doesn't seem to mind.
George You don't think that Jessica would condone what's going on between you and Wendy on a Wendy—on a Wednesday night if she *really* knew about it?
Brian What do you mean "if she really knew"? You were the one who told her.

George is silent. Brian peers at him, anxiously

George—you *did* tell her, didn't you?
George Well ... not exactly, no.
Brian What do you mean "not exactly, no"? She told me that you told her.
George Oh, yes. I told her all right. But I didn't tell her ... what you *think* I told her.
Brian Then what *did* you tell her?

Wendy arrives with a large whisky for George

Wendy Whisky!
George Thanks. (*He takes it*)
Brian George?
George Cheers!

Jessica returns with the flowers in a vase

Jessica There! Don't they look beautiful? (*She sets the vase down and notices George*) Oh, yes, George—that's much better. (*To Brian*)

George came home in some ridiculous suit he'd got from the Oxfam
shop.

Brian What? (*He looks at George in amused surprise*)

Jessica Wendy, would you like to come and give me a hand in the kitchen?

Wendy Yes, of course.

Jessica (*to the others*) We shan't be very long. (*Seeing George about to
drink*) Do see that *Brian* has a drink, won't you, George? (*She turns at
the door*) And please help yourselves to the nuts.

She and Wendy go out into the kitchen

Brian turns to George urgently

Brian Well? What *did* you tell her about me and Wendy?

George What *could* I tell her? I—I simply reinforced what you'd already
said.

Brian What was that?

George That Wendy was a Red Cross nurse.

Brian Oh, my God...!

George Well, I could hardly tell Jessica that I'd been lending you our flat
to have an affair in, could I? Women are funny about that sort of thing.

Brian (*reflectively*) I *thought* she was being awfully understanding about
it... Wait a minute, though. Why should Jessica think that I *needed*
nursing?

George Because I told her you were ill. Dicky heart.

Brian Oh, that's nice. That's very nice. Now, every time I make a move
she'll think I'm going to fall over! Well, you were right. I *am* ill. And
after this I probably *will* need nursing. Especially if Hilary finds out! Do
you mind if I use your bathroom? I think I'm going to be sick.

He stumbles out to the bathroom

*George goes quickly to look under the sofa again. He cannot see the
dressing-gown. He fetches Brian's umbrella and pokes it about under the
sofa. The doorbell rings. George reacts in alarm, causing the umbrella to
open up. He flails about with it on his way to the door and finally manages
to put it to rights. He puts it down and opens the front door*

*Hilary is there, carrying a large brown paper parcel. She smiles
brightly over the top of it*

George closes the door abruptly in her face. He thinks for a moment, then opens it again. Hilary is looking a little aggrieved

Hilary George...!

He gazes at her in horror as she walks into the room with her parcel. He closes the door and follows her, anxiously

George You're not coming here!
Hilary Yes, I am.
George Not tonight.
Hilary Yes.
George No!
Hilary Don't be silly. I'm here.
George Yes, you're here, but you're not supposed to be. You're supposed to be elsewhere, and elsewhere isn't here.
Hilary You said it was all arranged for tonight. In *your* flat for a change.
George When did I say that?
Hilary On the telephone. When I rang last night. Don't you remember?
George I was in my underwear last night. I can't remember what I say when I'm in my underwear.
Hilary Well, I can. And that was it. So here I am.

She sits on the sofa with the parcel on her knee. He glances, anxiously, towards the kitchen

George You can't come in here and sit down with a parcel!
Hilary Why not?
George It's—it's not convenient!

She looks at him patiently

Hilary Why don't you take this and give me a drink?
George You can't stay here!
Hilary George darling, do relax. You're relaxed when you're with me in *my* flat. Why can't you be relaxed when I'm with you in *your* flat? Do take this. It's awfully heavy.
George Oh. Right.

He goes to her reluctantly. She gets up and hands him the parcel. He stands there for a moment, uncertainly. Then he smiles

You ... you didn't have to bring me a present.

Hilary It isn't a present.

George Oh? What is it, then?

Hilary All your clothes, of course.

George What?! (*He throws the parcel back to her, abruptly*) I don't want it! Suppose somebody comes in and finds it?

Hilary Well, it's better to find your clothes in *your* flat than your clothes in *my* flat.

George starts to push her around the end of the sofa towards the front door

George Look—you go home! I'll try and join you there later on. It'll be much more peaceful there.

Hilary It seems very peaceful *here*.

George That's only the calm before the storm! Brian told me you were going out tonight.

Hilary Yes. I am. I'm coming here. To see you. (*She escapes from him and notices the dishes of nuts, etc*) Ah... You put out some nuts and things. How sweet. I think that's very nice. I'm quite touched. I shall have to do that next Wednesday when *you* come to see *me*.

Brian returns from the bathroom, talking as he comes in

Brian George, we'll have to do something about— (*He sees Hilary*) Oh, my God! (*He turns and goes straight out again*)

Hilary is frozen. She thinks she is seeing things. She looks at George. He smiles nervously, and shrugs

Hilary George...

George Y-y-yes?

Hilary Did you see that?

George H'm? See what?

Hilary What's Brian doing here?

George Brian? I didn't see any Brian.

Hilary Don't be ridiculous! Did you *know* Brian was going to be here?

George Yes, but I didn't know that *you* were going to be here!

Hilary (*alarmed*) Whatever's he going to think—finding me here with you?

George That's the least of his problems.

Brian's head appears furtively from the bathroom. He takes some time to move down to the sofa

Brian Sorry about that. I left the tap running in the bathroom. There are two. Not two running. Two taps. One blue and one red. One left and one right. And I left it running. The red one. (*He pretends to see Hilary for the first time and goes to her with a big smile*) Hullo, darling! I haven't seen you since this morning. I thought you said you were going out tonight?
Hilary Yes. I was. I did. I am.
Brian (*puzzled*) Sorry?
Hilary Well, I *am* out, aren't I?
Brian (*blankly*) Yes. (*Suddenly*) I say, what a very big parcel!

Hilary clutches the parcel to her bosom and backs away from him, nervously, to below the sofa

Hilary You can't have it!
Brian I don't want it.
Hilary That's all right, then. (*But she continues to hold on to the parcel, protectingly*) I... I expect you're wondering what I'm doing here.
George No, he isn't! It never crossed his mind. Did it, Brian? You never thought about it, did you?
Brian Don't be daft. I know what she's doing here.
George (*warily*) Do you?
Brian Of course I do. She's delivering a parcel. (*To Hilary*) Who is it for?
Hilary (*frozen*) What?
Brian The parcel.
Hilary Oh, it's ... er...
George Old clothes! Here—let me take them. (*He takes the parcel from Hilary*) It's very good of you, Hilary. She often brings old clothes here, you know. And I take them on to the Oxfam shop.
Brian The one you got your suit from?
George Yes.
Brian You must be supporting half the Third World by now.
George Well—I've got them, Hilary.
Hilary What?

George (*pointedly*) The old clothes. The old clothes for Oxfam. In the parcel. I've got them. So you can go. I mean, there's no point in your hanging about here, is there?

Brian (*eager to be rid of her, also*) Yes—you've probably got things you want to do at home.

Hilary (*eager to go*) Yes! I have! Masses! So I'll go home and do them.

Hilary sets off below Brian, heading, gratefully, towards the front door. The men are glad to be getting rid of her

But Jessica sails in from the kitchen and comes face-to-face with Hilary

They are equally surprised to see each other. Brian and George turn to each other in despair

Jessica Hilary!

Jessica turns slowly to look at Brian. He avoids her eyes elaborately and turns away. She looks at George. He hides behind the parcel. She looks back towards the kitchen, remembering her promise not to mention the Red Cross nurse to Hilary. Finally, she turns again to Hilary and smiles a big, delighted smile

Well. I'm *so* glad you were able to get here after all.

Hilary looks at her, bewildered. The men are frozen

Hilary W-what?

Jessica turns to look at George. He cowers behind the parcel

Jessica George...!

George (*peering nervously from behind the parcel*) Yes?

Jessica Get Hilary a drink and offer her some nuts.

George Yes. Right. (*But he remains poised with the parcel*)

Jessica George and I wanted you to come to dinner tonight, but Brian said you were going out.

Hilary Yes. I ... I was.

Jessica But you changed your mind?

Hilary Not exactly, no. (*She glances at George*)

Jessica Never mind. You're here now and we're delighted that you were able to make it. Do sit down.

Hilary Oh. Thanks. (*She sits down, apprehensively, on the sofa*)

Jessica Brian—isn't it wonderful that Hilary was able to make it, after all?

Brian Yes. Delightful. (*He goes to her, anxiously*) Look, Jessica, there's something I——

Jessica We'll have such a lot to talk about during dinner.

Brian looks apprehensive

George, why do you keep hiding behind that parcel? Hilary's waiting for her drink.

George Yes. Right.

He remains where he is. Hilary looks at him with a nervous smile. Jessica speaks confidentially to Brian

Jessica I'll leave *you* to explain the Red Cross nurse.

Brian is appalled at the prospect. Jessica turns to the others

You will excuse me, won't you? There's something simmering in the kitchen.

She goes out to the kitchen

Brian is thinking hard, trying to find a way out. Hilary smiles at George

Hilary George, how sweet of you *and* Jessica to invite me to dinner tonight.

George (*nervously*) Yes. It was, wasn't it?

Brian has thought of a way out and crosses urgently to George, who is hiding behind the parcel

Brian Now, look here, George—you can't spend the entire evening standing about with a parcel. Why don't you go and put the old clothes away somewhere?

Hilary Yes. You don't want to leave them lying about, do you?
George No fear!
Brian What?
George I'll take them upstairs. Pour your wife a drink, will you, Brian?
Brian Yes. Of course.
George I shan't be long.

He scuttles out upstairs with the parcel

Brian watches him go, then assumes a casual air and goes to the drinks

Brian Sherry, darling?
Hilary Yes, please.

Brian casts a look towards the kitchen and pours a sherry

Brian Poor old George...
Hilary What?
Brian He's in a bit of a state tonight.
Hilary Really? I hadn't noticed.

Brian overdoes his astonishment

Brian You hadn't noticed! Good Lord. He's been dancing about like a tom on the tiles. (*He arrives with the sherry*)
Hilary Thanks. (*She takes it*)

Brian casts another glance towards the stairs, to make sure George is not returning, and then sits beside Hilary, highly confidentially

Brian Mind you, it's not surprising. Under the circumstances.
Hilary Can I have a nut?
Brian (*put off his stride*) What? Oh. Yes. Right. (*He passes her the nuts*)
Hilary Thanks. (*She munches, contentedly*)

Brian glances again towards the stairs, then—

Brian You see, darling ... there are things you don't know about George.
Hilary There are things *you* don't know about him, either.

Brian What?
Hilary (*innocently*) Well, you can't know *everything*, can you, darling?
Brian Well, I *do* know that old George has got himself a girlfriend!

Hilary chokes on the nuts, thinking Brian knows about her and George. She sips some sherry and gradually recovers

Hilary W-w-what do you mean?
Brian (*smugly*) Oh, yes. I know all about it.
Hilary (*nervously*) You—you do?
Brian Oh, yes. But, whatever happens—*Jessica* mustn't know.
Hilary No! Of course not!
Brian So you won't tell her, will you?
Hilary Not likely! (*Fearfully*) How did *you* get to know?
Brian (*inventing wildly*) Ah—well—you see—he told me all about it. Man-to-man.
Hilary (*appalled*) *George* told you?
Brian Yes.
Hilary And you don't mind?
Brian (*puzzled*) Why should *I* mind?
Hilary (*outraged*) Brian! You're not even jealous!
Brian What?
Hilary I thought at least you'd be jealous!
Brian Why should *I* be jealous? *I'm* not his wife!
Hilary What?
Brian (*persevering, relentlessly*) Anyway—the point is—George's girlfriend ... is here tonight!
Hilary Yes. I know...
Brian Out there.
Hilary What...?
Brian In the kitchen.

Brian sits back, confident that he has covered his tracks. Hilary is now completely confused

Hilary No, darling. No—that's his wife—Jessica. Jessica is George's wife. *She*'s in the kitchen.
Brian So is George's girlfriend.
Hilary No, she isn't! (*She laughs*)

Brian I tell you, she's out there in the kitchen! And her name ... is Wendy.
Hilary (*her laugh dying*) *Wendy?*
Brian Yes.

Hilary's confusion gives way to a dawning suspicion about George

Hilary Are you trying to tell me that George has got a girlfriend called
Wendy?
Brian Yes!
Hilary (*livid*) Well, *I* didn't know that!
Brian Why should you? Anyway, you'll meet her in a minute.

Hilary is furious at (apparently) being two-timed by George

Hilary Oh, will I really? Well, you just wait till I see George...!
Brian Look—there's nothing for *you* to get into a state about——
Hilary Oh, yes, there is...!

Brian is now alarmed that Hilary is going to speak out of turn

Brian Look—you mustn't say anything to George!
Hilary Why not?
Brian Well ... he'd be embarrassed.
Hilary Well, why did you tell me, then?
Brian Ah—well—I *had* to tell you.
Hilary Why?
Brian Well ... because you might have misunderstood. You might have
wondered who Wendy was. And I didn't want you to wonder who
Wendy was...
Hilary (*abruptly*) I'd like a large Scotch!

Brian looks surprised

Brian You were drinking sherry.
Hilary (*loudly*) Well, I'm drinking Scotch now!

Brian is at a loss to understand her reactions

Brian Ah. Yes. Right.

He scuttles away to get a large whisky and a small jug of water

George comes downstairs and moves down to left of the sofa

Hilary looks at him, coldly, as he approaches

Hilary Ah! There you are, George!

George reacts, surprised by her tone

George What?
Hilary (*glaring at him*) Well? When are you going to introduce us? I'm simply longing to meet her.
George Meet who?
Hilary Wendy, of course!

Brian looks worried

George W-Wendy?
Hilary Yes! W-Wendy! She's in the kitchen.
George Ah. Yes. That's right. W-Wendy's in the kitchen with J-Jessica.

Brian intervenes with the large glass of whisky

Brian Whisky!
George You don't drink whisky.
Hilary I do *now*!

Brian and George look on in astonishment as Hilary downs the large whisky without taking a breath. Then Brian offers the small jug, helpfully

Brian Water?

Hilary ignores this. Brian shrugs and puts the jug down. Hilary puts down her empty glass decisively and rises to glare at George

Hilary Perhaps I'd better *not* stay to dinner. After all, I wasn't expected and there are *four* of you already. Aren't there, George?
George Well—yes—as a matter of fact there are. But we've plenty to go around.

Hilary Yes, I bet you have! (*The effects of the whisky hit her a little and she sits down again*)

George is totally bewildered by Hilary's changed attitude to him. Brian cannot understand why Hilary is reacting so vehemently to George having a girlfriend

George Is ... is everything all right?
Hilary (*snapping*) Oh, yes! Everything's fine!
George Oh, good. I just wondered. (*He tries to think what the hell is the matter with her*)
Hilary Oh, yes... You see—Brian has told me all about Wendy.

Brian looks appalled; George astonished

George He has?
Brian Hilary—darling—I did ask you not to say anything!
George (*to Brian*) Good Lord! You didn't *really* tell her, did you?

Hilary looks at George, amazed by this apparent admission of guilt

Hilary Oh, yes. He told me all right.
George And you don't mind? About Wendy.

Hilary shrugs, the wronged woman appearing to be indifferent

Hilary Why should *I* mind? It's nothing to do with *me*, is it? (*She looks at him pityingly*) I think it's rather amusing.
George Amusing?
Hilary And quite pathetic.
George But you don't mind?
Hilary Not in the least!
George Really? Good Lord. (*To Brian*) That's all right, then, isn't it, Brian?

Brian goes, hastily, to George, fearful of the conversation proceeding any further

Brian Look—I think this is all a bit embarrassing. I'd rather we didn't talk about it any more, if you don't mind.

Hilary Don't worry. I'm sure George doesn't want to talk about it, either. Do you, George?

George Well, after all, Brian is a friend of mine. (*He puts his arm around Brian, fraternally*)

None of this makes much sense to Hilary, who looks puzzled

Jessica comes in from the kitchen. Wendy follows her

Jessica Dinner won't be very long. I do hope you've all been helping yourselves to the nuts. Brian, perhaps *you*'d like to do the introductions? (*She waves, vaguely, towards Wendy*)

Brian is far from keen

Brian Well, I—er——

Hilary That won't be necessary. I've heard *all* about Wendy. (*She goes across to Wendy, who watches her approach, apprehensively*)

Wendy Have you?

Jessica (*to Brian*) Has she?

Hilary How do you do, Wendy.

They shake hands

I'm Brian's wife.

Wendy Oh, my God! I thought you weren't going to be here!

Jessica You've told Hilary all about Wendy, then, Brian?

Brian Er—yes. I think so...

Hilary (*to Jessica, surprised*) You mean *you* know about her, as well?

Jessica Yes, of course! Isn't she splendid?

Hilary looks bewildered by Jessica's (apparently) tolerant attitude to George having a girlfriend

Hilary *You* didn't tell her, did you, Brian?

Jessica No, no. George told me all about her.

Hilary looks at George, astonished

Hilary You told your own wife?

George Well, I had to give her some sort of explanation, didn't I?

Jessica Yes. After all, I *had* found them together.

Hilary (*to Jessica*) And you're quite happy about Wendy? (*Meaning being George's girlfriend*)

Jessica Yes. Of course. And I hope *you* will be, too. (*Meaning being Brian's nurse*)

Hilary Me?

Jessica Well, apparently she's always there when he needs her.

Hilary But that's got nothing to do with *me*! What George gets up to is entirely his affair.

Jessica is finding the water getting deeper and tries to remain afloat

Jessica Well, it is rather different for George, isn't it? After all, *he* doesn't go jogging, does he? So that's bound to reduce the risk.

Wendy (*looking up, puzzled*) What risk?

Brian almost yells at Wendy, desperately anxious to keep the cat safely in the bag

Brian Wendy—this is Hilary! Hilary is my wife!

Wendy Yes. I know.

Brian She's staying for dinner!

Wendy Is she?

Brian Yes. (*Pointedly*) *You* don't have to stay for dinner, if you don't want to. You can drink up and go. Now! If you want to.

Wendy Yes, I think I *do* want to... (*She finishes her drink quickly*)

Jessica We wouldn't dream of letting you go now. Would we, George?

George Wouldn't we?

Jessica Of course we wouldn't!

George Ah. I didn't know that.

Hilary I'm sure George wants her to stay.

She gives him an icy look, which he does not understand

Brian But if Wendy doesn't want to stay, I don't think we should force her. Do you, George?

George No, certainly not!

Jessica (*appalled by their manners*) How can you both be so unfeeling and inconsiderate? I wouldn't dream of letting Wendy go. It's a very good thing that there are people like her left in the world. She does a wonderful job. She brings comfort and succour to those in need, and I think we should all be grateful to her for what she does.

An impressive pause. Hilary is feeling the effects of the whisky

Hilary (*seething*) What the hell *does* she do?

Jessica hesitates, surprised at this outburst but not wishing to give away a confidence

Jessica What?
Hilary What *is* it that Wendy does that's so *wonderful*?
Jessica Well ... I—I don't think it's up to *me* to tell you. If Brian wants to put you in the picture, then that's his affair.
Hilary Brian? What's it got to do with Brian? (*She looks at him*)

Brian cowers, nervously

Jessica But I certainly have no intention of breaking my word and betraying a confidence. (*She smiles, reassuringly, at Brian*)
Brian Thank you, Jessica.
Hilary Well, come on, then, Wendy! *You* tell us! What exactly *is* it that you do so wonderfully?
Wendy (*modestly*) Well, it's not very exciting...
Hilary Oh, I'm sure you *make* it exciting! Eh, George?
George (*puzzled*) Sorry?
Wendy I work at Boon and Prentiss. I'm a cash desk operative.
Jessica (*astounded*) Don't be ridiculous!
Wendy (*persisting*) I'm a cash desk operative!
Jessica No, you're not!
Wendy I should know what I am!
Jessica You should, but you obviously don't. I can see that gin only makes you forgetful.
Wendy (*loudly*) I'm a cash desk operative!

Jessica turns and moves, thoughtfully, to George. He cowers, waiting for the inevitable

Jessica George...
George H'm?
Jessica You said Wendy was a Red Cross nurse. I haven't seen many
nurses behind the check-out at Boon and Prentiss.
Wendy Let's face it—do I *look* like a nurse?
Jessica Well, perhaps you're not exactly Florence Nightingale. But they
do come in all shapes and sizes. (*She turns on George*) It's all *your* fault!
George Yes. I thought it would be...!

Brian crosses desperately to Hilary and grabs her by the hand

Brian Come on, Hilary!
Hilary Where are we going?
Brian To the bathroom! I'll show you George's bathroom.

He starts to lead her away, but she resists

Hilary I don't want to see George's bathroom. This is *far* more
interesting.
Brian George—why don't you say something?
George I can't remember the Lord's Prayer...

*Jessica has been thinking deeply, trying to work something out, and now
speaks slowly and carefully*

Jessica But Wendy—if you're *not* a nurse ... what on earth were you
doing bringing Brian back here last night when he felt faint in the middle
of jogging?

A dreadful silence. Jessica—at last—realizes. And so does Hilary

Oh...! Ah. I see...
Hilary So do I...! (*She looks stonily at Brian*)

Jessica knows that she has well and truly put her foot in it

Jessica Oh, dear... (*She tries to carry it off and speaks rather too brightly
and cheerfully*) Well! Dinner won't be very long!

Nobody reacts

I'll just pop upstairs and get the table napkins! And then we'll all have dinner. (*She backs, awkwardly, towards the stairs*) I bet you're all longing for dinner. Do help yourselves to the nuts.

Her heartiness deflates like a balloon and she stumbles out up the stairs

For a moment nobody dares to speak. They all stare ahead, seeing nothing. Then Hilary drifts, thoughtfully, below the sofa. Brian cowers, waiting for the explosion

Hilary Brian?
Brian (*nervously*) Er—y-y-yes?
Hilary I thought Wendy was *George's* girl-friend.
Wendy ⎱ (*together*) What?!
George ⎰
Brian Ah. Yes. Well...
George *Mine?* Whatever gave you that idea?
Hilary Oh, just something somebody said. (*She looks icily at Brian*)

George now understands why she was behaving so strangely to him

George Oh, I see! So *that's* why you were being so— (*He breaks off*)
Brian Why she was being so what?
George (*hastily*) Nothing! Nothing at all!

Hilary takes Brian's arm and speaks to him cosily, in mock concern

Hilary You poor darling. You never told me you felt faint when you were out jogging. You were so brave. I'd never have guessed.
Brian Well, I was feeling all right by the time I got home.
Hilary Yes, I *bet* you were! (*She looks at Wendy*) And how about the Red Cross nurse? Was everything all right for you, too?
Wendy (*unhappily*) No, it wasn't. We had the *coq au vin* and then we went home...

Hilary starts to laugh. She pats Brian's face, delightedly

Hilary Oh, darling—you had *coq au vin*...! How nice!
Wendy (*surprised*) Aren't you going to be angry?

Hilary There's no point in being angry.

Wendy (*persisting*) Aren't you going to divorce him?

Brian You keep out of this!

Hilary Why should I divorce him? I like him. You know—I'd no idea that *this* was what people meant by jogging. Just think of it. All over the country there are hundreds of people racing about in track suits. (*Thoughtfully*) Perhaps they're *all* doing this...

Wendy I think I'd better be going... (*She starts to go*)

Hilary Don't be silly. Dinner's ready.

Wendy I'm not very hungry...

Hilary Jessica will be very upset if you leave now. She invited you to dinner—and you're jolly well going to stay. Come along! We'll go and see to the vegetables.

She leads Wendy towards the kitchen. Wendy is still completely over-whelmed by Hilary's tolerance

Wendy I must say, I think you're being wonderful about this. Absolutely wonderful. I really can't think why you're being so understanding.

Hilary (*smiling secretly*) You'd never believe it if I told you.

She grins at George and goes out to the kitchen with Wendy

Brian (*sinking mournfully on to the sofa*) Well ... that's that, eh? What a pity. It was such a nice little arrangement, wasn't it?

George It certainly was...! (*Sitting beside him*) I shouldn't worry, if I were you. Give it a couple of weeks. Then you can start all over again.

Brian What? Jogging and—er—?

George Why not? It's too good an alibi to throw away, isn't it?

Brian Oh, no. No chance. Hilary would never fall for that one again.

George gives a little secret smile

George Oh, I dunno. I have a funny sort of feeling that she *might*...

Jessica returns with the table napkins. She sees that Hilary and Wendy are not there

Jessica Oh? Have they gone?

Brian Only to the kitchen.

Jessica Oh, good. George—something quite extraordinary. You know that sports jacket you said you'd given to Oxfam...

George (*warily*) Y-yes?

Jessica I found it upstairs. Wrapped up in brown paper with your blue suit.

George Ah. Yes. Well, I—I suddenly missed the old jacket. I know *you* don't like it, but it is one of my favourites. So I—I phoned Hilary and asked her to pop into Oxfam and buy it back.

Jessica But your *suit* wasn't at Oxfam.

George No. That was at the cleaners.

Jessica So Hilary picked that up at the same time?

George Yes.

Jessica And wrapped the whole lot up in brown paper and brought them round here?

George Yes.

Jessica What a helpful girl she is. Well—I expect you're both dying for dinner?

The men do not look enthusiastic

Brian (*sheepishly*) Sorry, Jessica.

Jessica Sorry about dinner?

Brian No, no—about ... Wendy.

Jessica There's nothing to be sorry about. As a matter of fact, I'm rather relieved.

Brian Why?

Jessica Well, now at least I know how *this* came to be here.

Whereupon she produces his dressing-gown from a cupboard and holds it up. Brian stares at it

Brian That's my dressing-gown!

Jessica Yes. You must have left it here last night.

George looks glassy. Brian looks puzzled

Brian Where did you find it, then?

Jessica Where do you think? Here—under the sofa.

She drops the dressing-gown into his lap and goes out to the kitchen

A long pause. George shifts nervously. Brian is deep in thought, gazing at the dressing-gown. Finally...

Brian George...?
George Y-yes?
Brian How the hell did *my* dressing-gown get under *your* sofa?

A nasty pause. Brian looks at George, his suspicion starting

Well, George? What have you got to say?
George "Our Father which art in heaven, hallowed be Thy name..."

He escapes around the sofa and heads for the kitchen. Brian reacts and starts to follow him

Brian George...? George!

The telephone rings as Jessica comes in from the kitchen

Jessica All right. I'll get it.

George is moving into the kitchen, Brian following him

Brian George...! Wait a minute! George!

Jessica watches them go in surprise as she lifts the telephone receiver

They disappear into the kitchen

Jessica Hullo? ... Yes, I got back last night. ... (*She smiles happily*) Yes, of course, darling—Wednesday evening, same time as usual!

She replaces the receiver with a smile and walks on air towards the kitchen as—

—*the* CURTAIN *falls*

FURNITURE AND PROPERTY LIST

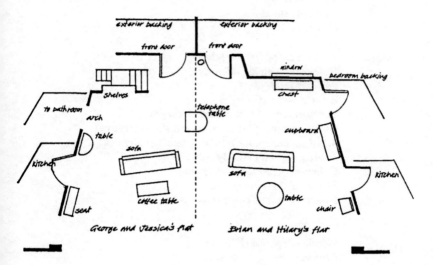

George and Jessica's flat

Brian and Hilary's flat

ACT I

On stage: **GEORGE AND JESSICA'S FLAT:**
Small modern sofa
Coffee table
Crescent table. *On it:* bowl of fruit
Padded bench seat
Bookshelves. *On them:* bottles of gin, sherry, tonic water,
   various glasses, books, ornaments, stereo music-centre
On walls: modern mirror, pictures
Telephone table. *On it:* letters, **George**'s glasses, modern
   telephone
Carpet

BRIAN AND HILARY'S FLAT:
Small Victorian sofa
Oval coffee table
Antique chest
Dining chair

Cupboard. *On it:* framed photograph of **Brian**, 2 martini
  glasses
On walls: period mirror, pictures, leopard skin
Window curtains (closed)
Telephone table
Umbrella stand
Carpet

Off stage: Perfume atomiser (**Wendy**)
Ice-bucket with ice (**Wendy**)
Perfume atomiser (**Hilary**)
Bicycle pump (**George**)
Bottle of red wine, wrapped (**George**)
Glass jug containing cocktail and stirrer (**Hilary**)
Small suitcase, duty-free bag, handbag (**Jessica**)
Jessica's apron (**Wendy**)
George's dressing-gown (**Brian**)
Martini glass (**Hilary**)
Brian's dressing-gown (**George**)
Oven gloves (**Hilary**)
Tray (**Wendy**)
Mobile telephone (**Hilary**)
Pyjama trousers (**George**)
Glass of wine (**Hilary**)
Tray. *On it:* plate of *coq au vin*, knife, fork, napkin (**Hilary**)
Tray. *On it:* plate of *coq au vin*, knife, fork, napkin, pepper
  and salt (**George**)

Personal: **Wendy**: wrist-watch
Hilary: wrist-watch
George: yellow safety harness, yellow bicycle clips,
  wrist-watch
Jessica: wrist-watch

ACT II

Strike: *From* **George** *and* **Jessica**'s *flat:*
Apple, book, dirty glasses, **Brian**'s dressing-gown, **Jessica**'s
  handbag and coat, duty-free bag, tray with plate of *coq au*
  vin, etc.

From **Brian** *and* **Hilary's** *flat:*
Bicycle clips, dirty glass

Set:	*In* **Brian** *and* **Hilary**'s *flat:*
	Window curtains open
	Umbrella, briefcase, papers for **Brian**
	Coffee-pot, milk-jug, sugar-bowl, 2 cups, 2 saucers,
	2 spoons on cupboard top

In **George** *and* **Jessica**'s *flat:*
Brian's dressing-gown in cupboard
Small jug of water

Off stage: Cup of coffee (**George**)
   Towels (**Hilary**)
   Carrier bag (**Hilary**)
   Cup of coffee (**Jessica**)
   Latchkey (**Hilary**)
   Tray. *On it:* dishes of nuts, crisps, etc. (**Jessica**)
   Umbrella, briefcase, bunch of flowers (**Brian**)
   Vase of flowers (**Jessica**)
   Large brown paper parcel (**Hilary**)
   Table napkins (**Jessica**)

Personal: **Brian**: bicycle clips in pocket, wrist-watch
   George: wrist-watch, key

LIGHTING PLOT

Property fittings required: lamps as needed
Interior. Two living-rooms. The same scene throughout

ACT I   Evening

To open: Black-out

Cue 1   As CURTAIN rises   (Page 2)
           Bring up lights in **George** *and* **Jessica**'s *flat—general
           interior lighting*

Cue 2   As **Brian** and **Wendy** run out   (Page 7)
           Black-out in **George** *and* **Jessica**'s *flat. Bring up lights
           in* **Brian** *and* **Hilary**'s *flat—general interior lighting*

Cue 3   **George** follows **Hilary**   (Page 13)
           Black-out in **Brian** *and* **Hilary**'s *flat. Bring up lights
           in* **George** *and* **Jessica**'s *flat*

Cue 4   **Wendy**: "…central heating's failed again?"   (Page 21)
           Black-out in **George** *and* **Jessica**'s *flat. Bring up lights
           in* **Brian** *and* **Hilary**'s *flat*

Cue 5   **Jessica** follows **Hilary** into the kitchen   (Page 31)
           Black-out in **Brian** *and* **Hilary**'s *flat. Bring up lights
           in* **George** *and* **Jessica**'s *flat*

Cue 6   **Wendy**: "All right—I'll answer it".   (Page 37)
           Bring up lights in **Brian** *and* **Hilary**'s *flat*

Cue 7   **Hilary** goes into the kitchen   (Page 39)
           Fade out lights in **Brian** *and* **Hilary**'s *flat*

Cue 8   **Jessica**: "…my clothes tonight, do I?"   (Page 43)
           Black-out in **George** *and* **Jessica**'s *flat. Bring up lights
           in* **Brian** *and* **Hilary**'s *flat*

| *Cue* 9 | As **Hilary** goes out to the kitchen | (Page 45) |
| | *Bring up lights in* **George** *and* **Jessica**'s *flat* | |

| *Cue* 10 | **George**: *"Coq au vin!"* | (rage 47) |
| | *Black-out in both flats* | |

ACT II   Morning and evening

To open: Black-out

Cue 11	As C*urtain* rises	(Page 48)
	Bring up lights in **Brian** *and* **Hilary**'s *flat—general*	
	interior lighting	

| *Cue* 12 | As **Hilary** dials | (Page 52) |
| | *Bring up lights in* **George** *and* **Jessica**'s *flat* | |

| *Cue* 13 | As **Hilary** hangs up | (Page 52) |
| | *Fade out lights in* **Brian** *and* **Hilary**'s *flat* | |

| *Cue* 14 | As **Jessica** goes towards the kitchen | (Page 57) |
| | *Crossfade to* **Brian** *and* **Hilary**'s *flat* | |

| *Cue* 15 | As **Hilary** goes to the bedroom | (Page 57) |
| | *Crossfade to* **George** *and* **Jessica**'s *flat* | |

| *Cue* 16 | **Jessica** sighs and heads for the kitchen | (Page 63) |
| | *Crossfade to* **Brian** *and* **Hilary**'s *flat* | |

Cue 17	**Brian** starts to follow **Hilary** into the kitchen	(Page 68)
	Black-out in **Brian** *and* **Hilary**'s *flat, then bring up*	
	lights in **George** *and* **Jessica**'s *flat*	

Note: On the last cue spread the area of lighting into part of the other flat in order to increase the acting area in **George** and **Jessica**'s flat for the final scene

EFFECTS PLOT

ACT I

ACT II

Lightning Source UK Ltd.
Milton Keynes UK
UKOW05f0230170215

246377UK00001B/37/P